Georgia

Alwin
Schockemöhle

Alwin Schockemöhle

by ALWIN SCHOCKEMÖHLE

with ULRICH KAISER

Translated by
STELLA and VERNON HUMPHRIES

Foreword by
DAVID BROOME

ANGUS AND ROBERTSON · PUBLISHERS

ANGUS & ROBERTSON . PUBLISHERS
London . Sydney . Melbourne . Singapore . Manila

First published by Angus and Robertson (UK) Ltd,
2, Fisher Street, London, WC1, in 1977

Copyright © Copress-Verlag 1976

Copyright Extra Text © Hippo Media 1977

Copyright English Translation © Angus and Robertson (UK) Ltd, 1977

ISBN 0 207 95774 6

Typesetting by Ronset Limited, Darwen, Lancashire.

Printed and bound in Great Britain by
Butler & Tanner Ltd, Frome and London

Contents

Foreword

FOREWORD BY DAVID BROOME

When you meet Alwin Schockemöhle the first thing you realise is what a gentleman he is. When you compete against him you begin to understand the standard of horsemanship that has made him the most successful Grand Prix winner of all time, and, should you ever be successful enough to beat him, you then learn how true sportsmen should behave. When you combine all these qualities together with a shrewd business brain and a sharp wit, you realise what an asset Alwin is to the show jumping world.

This book not only tells of Alwin's early life and how he became involved in show jumping, of his successes and defeats, and of the highs and lows of a much acclaimed personality; but it tells most candidly what goes on behind the scenes. It is a very rare and personal insight into the inspired mind of a man with a very intellectual outlook on life. He reveals with complete honesty the truth behind the glamour of the immaculate scarlet riding jacket and that reward lap of honour. It is only by reading his autobiography that we realise that there is so much more to this man than his talent and determination, and that there is far more to success than just dreaming about it.

I think this book needs to be read by everyone regardless of whether they are interested in or connected with horses. Basically, people like to know the truth—we are all rather nosey and we all love to know what makes a person tick! Although I have known Alwin for twenty years, after reading his book I now feel that I know him even better. I am sure that by reading his interesting and entertaining autobiography you, too, will feel that you know him personally.

I sincerely hope you will enjoy the following pages as much as I did.

Personality

Alwin Schockemöhle is one of the greatest personalities ever in the world of horsemen. It is difficult to put into words why this man has become a legend in his own lifetime. Nobody sits a horse like he does. Prophets of the old school are forever denouncing his methods. They have attacked him for the use of the draw-rein but they have been proved wrong. Alwin bent the laws of horsemanship to suit his own theories; he adopted the classic riding style to his own bodybuild. The results are not always aesthetically pleasing, but his horses understand him and successes achieved are overpowering arguments for his vision.

Typical of Alwin's individuality is the fact that it is nearly impossible to imitate him. Many a horseman has taken tips from him but nobody in international competitions rides just as he does. His style of riding, his intelligence, his sensitivity, his flair, his dedication and professionalism have made Alwin Schockemöhle the unique personality he is.

Alwin Schockemöhle was born on May 29th 1937 in the village of Osterbrock. His parents were farmers there. Their main income however was earned by dealing in stallions. So one can see that Alwin's knowledge of horses probably was handed down to him by his father. His father was himself quite an accomplished jumper and jockey. Alwin too had experience in horse racing. As a 12 year old boy he achieved his first success with his mare in the village of Quakenbrück. Alwin also tells us that he at that time, was the proud owner of a piebald mare named Mädel. With this horse he took part in and won at various jump, dressage and combination events.

Later the family returned to Mühlen in Oldenburg, the original family home. The reason that father Schockemöhle had taken on the farm in Osterbrock was a difference of opinion with *his* father; luckily all was happily settled later and the family returned to the old home – the farmhouse under the tall oaktrees in Mühlen. This farm had been in the family for over 400 years.

Alwin Schockemöhle:

"The old farm burned down in 1952. We rebuilt the whole thing to its original design from the outside, and only altered the interior. In the main building my mother and brother Paul now live. The two wings which stand at rightangles to the main building are now the stables. Next to that is the riding hall and behind this are two more open horse boxes and a smaller riding school. The main stable burned down in 1970 while I was at Hickstead. There were 6,000 bales of straw in the loft. Luckily all the horses were brought to safety and eight weeks after this disaster the whole thing was rebuilt again."

Near the old farm and stables Alwin has built his new villa, separated from the other buildings by spruce and rhododendrums. The entrance hall with a cosy nook and the main sitting room bear witness to his good taste. On either side of the fireplace there are some silver cupboards; otherwise there are no cups or prizes to be seen. They are all in the old farm.

Alwin constantly crosses from the villa to the stables to supervise his staff and horses.

Now and again he will still ride a horse, but much less often than in the past. Now he only rides the top horses or young horses with handling difficulties.

His back injury prevents him from maintaining his former rhythm of work.

Alwin Schockemöhle:

"The ligaments around my spinal column are worn out and one vertebra has been damaged. The good Lord did not design man's back for sitting on a horse for seven hours a day and then immediately afterwards rushing around in cars. I am in constant discomfort and now and again feel a searing pain but my performance is not affected by it. Every so often I have to miss a competition and I am under regular medical surveillance. I am not as strong as I used to be. On top of that I broke my right arm; it is crooked here just under my watch. It hurts me to lift heavy things. The times of lugging and trailing things about on the farm are over for good, I am afraid.

"When I was eighteen I took part in a bet. I had to carry four hundred pounds from the mill across the yard to the barn. That was two sacks of grain, of two hundred pounds each. One I put on my shoulders myself and the boys put the other one on top of the first one. I did win the bet, but now I have to be careful.

"I will stop taking part in competitions before it becomes noticeable that my performances are not what they used to be. I will notice that before anyone else does".

When Alwin made these remarks he was at the peak of his career. The "Champion Without Titles" had collected his titles two years before in the European Championships and the previous year in the Olympic Championships.

Warwick Rex finally brought him these titles after he had ridden famous horses like Freya, Freihert, Bacchus, Ferdl, Exact, Donald Rex, and Rex the Robber, for years. Warwick Rex, a horse once written off completely by a vet. *Alwin Schockemöhle:*

"That horse had been sold to Leon Melchior by Friedrich Ernst from Verden. The horse picked up some lung complaint and went back to Ernst for a while. I rang Stihl who had treated the animal and he told me Warwick was finished and incurably ill. But in the good dry air of Verden Warwick kept on improving in health. I have an idea that the degree of humidity in Zangersheide is higher than in Verden and that this affected the lungs of this fantastic horse. In any case I could have the horse with the proviso that I could return him if he did not stay healthy. I wanted to have a go because the potential of this horse is limitless. Over an obstacle of 1·60 metres (5ft 2ins) he does drop his legs because he does not need any technique at this height; only at 2 metres (6ft 6ins) will you see that he really has technique because only then does he need it.

"Warwick remained healthy and I had the ideal Olympic horse. His potential is simply enormous; he is careful but not too careful. The Robber was too careful. That kind of horse can be confused and may on occasion refuse in the middle of a difficult course. An Olympic horse must be unflappable. In Montreal people talked about a 'veterinary' top performance but that is nonsense.

Of course we looked after him well there; that goes without saying; but even after Montreal he proved himself more than once.

"In the months before Montreal we had a lot of bad luck. He had a virus infection and he went lame. When I had him in top condition again just in time for Montreal people could, of course, talk about a 'veterinary' top performance, but it was just a question of working up to optimum form using the correct methods. When I observed this improved fitness I geared my training schedules to his fitness and the result of all this is well known!"

In general Alwin Schockemöhle has his own ideas about veterinary care. He thinks it can be overdone now that nearly every one who takes care of a horse claims to be a fully qualified vet. He thinks that a lot of drugs, while not actually illegal, are used much too much.

"Some horses are just pumped full of the stuff and people do not realise the negative results in the long run because the horses age much more quickly," says Alwin. He therefore pleads for regulations to ensure that only qualified vets will be allowed as veterinary assistants.

The Family Home

The Schockemöhle farm has been let now to a tenant. He has built himself a house a stone's throw away, a really beautiful one with an overhanging thatched roof, big rooms and big windows. "You half expect the pheasants to stroll into the living room. No shooting is allowed round here." A serious-eyed little girl says "Good morning" politely, and a little mischief of a lad threatens you with his water pistol. There are three children altogether. Alwin himself is one of a family of four and the eldest of the boys. The farm was in a bad way when he invested his money in it. He was just twenty.

Among one's childhood recollections there are sometimes tiny and often fragmentary visual images which keep recurring as vividly as if they had happened yesterday. One of these, in Alwin Schockemöhle's case, goes back to the days when he still lived in the Emsland village of Osterbrock. It was during the last few months of the war, and he can still see himself driving full tilt in a two-wheeled trap, chased by the machine guns of low flying planes. Another memory, from a few years later, is of one of those crazy races which enthusiasts used to organise thereabouts. Someone had offered him the hardest-mouthed horse in the race. He was still a slip of a boy, but he won, although he had no boots and still wore short trousers. The inside skin of his legs near the knee was hanging down in shreds. But he won.

Alwin Schockemöhle:
"There were always horses around as long as I can remember. My father wasn't a hard man, although this may sound unusual for a farmer. He was more of an artist, a person who worried a lot about everyday things, and who sometimes simply had to find a safety valve. Even when times were bad, he always kept horses. He

11

loved them. This may seem exaggerated, but it's true. He really loved them. At first, he kept race horses and of course I rode. He didn't have to force me. I did it because it was fun, that was all. He was interested in half-breds. There was a great deal of racing on the smaller courses, with something going on almost every weekend. We always took our horses along and we always raced.

"In those days, when I was a boy, there wasn't so much regimentation. There were just horseshows, with jumping, dressage and racing too. Father was always buying a few race horses for himself. Many of them were injured or sick. He used to patch them up as best he could; he did this with great devotion and also with some success.

"It was then that I started competing in so-called pony races. Later on, there were the regional horse trials. At these I used to go in for everything, jumping, dressage, flat racing. It was tremendous fun – championships, cups and the like were still a long way away. And then suddenly Gustav Rau appeared on the scene. He invited me to a training course at Warendorf."

During the first half of this century, there was scarcely a German horseman whose riding career was not decisively affected by meeting Gustav Rau. He was born 28th February 1880 and died 5th December 1954, and he was a kind of father figure to them all. He was a man who was obviously endowed with clearsighted understanding of his profession, who never lost his sense of humour even when dealing with the inevitable red tape, a person whose tenacious originality is still acknowledged and respected today, an expert who even nowadays would have got rid of much that bedevils both riding and its jargon.

Gustav Rau, who was born in Paris, may be said to have been a conservative with a small "c". This didn't stop him from abolishing traditions when they were in danger of growing stale. He was respected for the clarity of his mind and not because of the office he held. Rau had in fact been earmarked for quite a different career, and it was as a journalist, when he was barely of age at the turn of the century, that the brilliance of his phrasing and his knowledgeability created something of a stir. In Germany today his textbooks and essays are still considered as standard works.

12

Gustav Rau became General Secretary of the German equestrian Olympic committee and he may be considered as the "inventor" of the new German style of riding. In 1933, he was appointed head of the Prussian stables. In 1943, the University of Bonn awarded him an honorary degree. After 1945, he revived equestrianism as a competitive sport on the basis of regional trials, and that at a time when the Germans had many other things to worry about besides riding.

A tall slim figure in a crumpled raincoat, with a half chewed cigar and thick spectacles, Gustav Rau was a man who could be caustic, sarcastic, even cynical. But when he said: "Come on, children, let me see you do it!", they did in fact "do it", no matter what he demanded of them. He was a man with an infallible eye for talent and for horses. On one occasion, probably at the beginning of the 1950's, he went up to the winner of the Vornholz contest and said: "Well done, my lad. You've a big future ahead of you!" Then turning to his wife, he added gruffly: "And do stop worrying, Herta!" The rider, a matter of fact young man, who even today hasn't quite mastered the art of winning instant popularity, muttered something noncomittal and turned back to his horse. His name was Hans Günter Winkler. A few years later he won an Olympic gold medal and followed it with several more.

Gustav Rau could express complex ideas more simply than most modern experts. Although this book is about a show jumper, it is not out of place to quote here Rau's half dozen maxims for dressage riding. Another good reason for doing so is that, according to German riding concepts, success as a show jumper is impossible without dressage schooling, and also because at that time, Alwin Schockemöhle was still a long way from becoming a show jumper.

According to Gustav Rau, these are the decisive factors for winning a really difficult competition such as the Dressage Grand Prix:

1. The greatest possible harmony between rider and horse, presenting a composite picture both stimulating in itself and pleasing to the eye, with no suggestion of strain or clumsiness.

2. The horse should move effortlessly, as if of his own

volition, with the rider using the bit very gently and for guidance only.

3. The rider should secure his effects with only invisible aids, never dominating the scene, but confining himself to being part of the total impression.

4. Clean, even movements in walking, trotting and cantering.

5. The horse must be able to change tempo with ease, and also to respond instantaneously to the rider's other demands; to take the smallest possible steps in rapid time and with the utmost concentration and, a moment later, to dart forward with all possible impulsion and then, just as easily, reduce speed once more and return again to the shortened tempo.

6. The natural ease of the whole performance which must leave the impression that these things present no difficulty, and that rider and horse need no effort to achieve them.

The whole exercise sounds, simple, obvious and graceful. Riding today might be much more popular if someone could translate the current obscure horsy jargon into straightforward up to date language.

The principal association for the breeding and trial of horses in Germany has donated a Gustav Rau medal as its highest distinction. It is awarded to those who have, by their special achievements, excelled as breeders, scientists, writers, judges, organisers or creators of new ideas in the field of horsebreeding and horse trials, in Germany or elsewhere.

Gustav Rau considered that the young man Alwin Schockemöhle was talented enough to ask him back to Warendorf time and again.

Alwin Schockemöhle:

"We were a good team in Warendorf in those days. Hermann Schridde was there and so were Reiner Klimke and Luetke-Westhuis. We spurred each other on. If one of us had mastered something better than the rest, the others practised and trained until they could do it too. I don't think there was ever anything like it again at Warendorf. We were young, we loved horses, we were crazy about riding, we all wanted to get to the top as quickly as possible, and we slaved away to achieve this. I spent at least eighteen months in all at Warendorf. Of course it wasn't a consecutive period. It used to be four weeks at Warendorf and four weeks at home. Gustav Rau asked me to come back time and again. General Niemack taught us dressage – he was an instructor there, and a good one too. At home, in between spells at Warendorf, I went with my father to local trials as before. There was racing, show jumping and dressage. I started winning.

"I could feel that the instruction at Warendorf was doing me good. At home, by yourself, you can only reach a certain standard. Thereafter, you need teachers from whom you can learn. But the intervening periods I spent at home were also beneficial, since I could immediately put my training into practice.

"Schridde, Klimke and I were considered at the time as the junior team for three-day eventing. I believe that this preparation was extraordinarily useful to us, because it was so varied. Klimke, who is one of the best dressage riders in the world today, rode in the three-day event at the 1960 Olympic Games in Rome. As for me, I had suddenly become a show jumper, practically overnight. In Verden, there was a biscuit and wafer manufacturer named Herr Freitag, who had his own stables for competition horses. Hermann Schridde went there first, but there seems to have been a certain difference of opinion later. At the Wiesbaden trials, we agreed that I should take over from him at Herr Freitag's. Hermann then returned to Warendorf, and I went to Verden where I remained for six or seven years."

It all sounds so simple – to "become a showjumper overnight" – just like that. Here was a man who in the years of his first successes did much more than merely gather friends about him. He was someone who, quite apart from his riding, used his cool business head to salvage the family estate; whose realism enabled him to see what line to pursue, what was feasible and was likely to be profitable, and who kept both feet so firmly on the ground that one can only smile at the description of him as an idealist. But is application to hard work a term of reproach? In those years, Alwin Schockemöhle worked like a slave, seeing to business here, there, and everywhere, riding early in the morning whilst others slept, or in the evening, when they were sitting comfortably at home.

Was he no more than highly capable? Was he merely lucky?

Alwin Schockemöhle:

"In those days I admired people like Winkler and Fritz Thiedemann. I used to sit glued to the radio whenever they were performing and the events were reported. I devoured newspapers and magazines with articles about them. Looking back, I consider this was perfectly normal. There was I in my Oldenburg village, and mad keen on equestrian sports, so I simply had to worship these celebrities. There are thousands of boys like this all over the world, raving about Beckenbauer, Muhammed Ali or Niki Lauda. That's what boys are like and I was one of them. On one occasion I scraped together all my pocket money so that I could go first to Münster and then to Dortmund. There I gazed with admiration at the great riders in the arena, and tried to learn something from them.

"How did I become a show jumper? And how did I get into the team that won the Olympic gold medal in Rome in 1960? And how did it happen that out of the blue I was allowed to ride with my idols Winkler and Thiedemann?

"What really must have started it was a meeting at the Theresien ground in Munich during the German Agricultural Show. I was one of the Oldenburg riding team – I was very green, and only eighteen or so. I hadn't taken part even in intermediate events in show jumping.

"Once our regional competitions were over, I wanted to sample life in the big city, Munich. For the first time in my life I went to a night club. There I met a girl who, for an eighteen-year-old like me, seemed the quintessence of feminine charm. She whispered in my ear that I should wait for her. I waited until five or six in the morning – the twenty D-marks I had had on me had long been spent. However, she didn't come, the bitch – probably she was sound asleep long before, whilst I paced up and down in front of the door, miserably cold, and people started going to work. Today I can only say: thank goodness she didn't turn up.

"I was staying in private digs – whoever went to hotels in 1955? – I returned to those digs, still wearing my best black suit. It had been my father's and had had to be

16

altered to fit me. It was my Sunday best. I was still wearing it when I drove out to the show ring. I must have looked ghastly.

"At the stables there I met a certain Herr Bolten who owned two horses, Adolar and Marsalla. I shall never forget them, great brutes they were, the East Prussian breed, bony, strong, hardmouthed. Actually Herr Bolten had a rider for them who, like me, had ridden in the previous trials, but for the Rhineland team. But this chap had walked out on Herr Bolten, and had gone with the others to Garmisch – probably on business or something like that. Herr Bolten was in trouble. He wanted his horses to compete, but he had no rider. Then I happened to cross his path. As I've said, I must have looked pretty washed out – I hadn't slept at all that night – but Herr Bolten asked me whether I'd like to ride his two horses for him. The mood I was in, I'd probably have said yes if someone had asked me to fly to the moon.

"These horses from the Rhineland team were much better schooled than ours from Oldenburg. They had already competed at intermediate and advanced trials. I agreed, for although I had no idea what I was in for, the attempt would cost me nothing financially and, for this once, I wanted to have a go. Of course, I was still wearing my black suit. So I went round to the tents where nearly everyone was still asleep and they must have thought I was out of my mind when I explained that I wanted to borrow riding breeches, a red coat and a pair of boots. I expect they only lent me the outfit so as to get rid of me as quickly as possible.

"There was a puissance competition and five times I tied for first place with Fritz Thiedemann who was riding Meteor. The final wall jump was 2·10 metres (7ft) high and there was I who had never in my life managed to clear more than 1·50 metres (5ft). I remember it as if it were yesterday. At the high-wide jump I had incurred one fault right in the middle, because I didn't know the routine. Even then I surprised myself, and of course I was a bit proud and happy. And tired, that goes without saying.

"I was in my seventh heaven. Suddenly people were saying that this fellow Schockemöhle had tied five times with the great Thiedemann. My name was in the papers, for in those days, any German rider who could shake the throne of Thiedemann and Winkler was bound to hit the headlines. There weren't nearly as many good riders then as there are today. After the show we too went off to Garmisch and celebrated. It didn't even occur to me that I ought to have been in bed long ago.

"Marsalla was then transferred to Herr Freitag's stud and very likely this played a part in the difference of opinion he had with Hermann Schridde later. Adolar was bought by François Poncet, the French diplomat. Suddenly these horses were of some value; in fact, any horse which came second or fourth to Thiedemann's was worth something in those days.

"That is the story of how I actually became a show jumper overnight. What happened after that is common knowledge. People believe that a successful rider can bring other horses to the same pitch of performance. All at once, several owners wanted me to school their horses – they made me offers by telephone. No doubt I made mistakes – but which boy of eighteen doesn't make mistakes?

"First of all though I went back to Warendorf and even there I was no longer considered as a three-day event man, but as a show jumper. Till then, I hadn't known it myself! The next few months were fairly hectic – one can almost say the next few years. I was overwhelmed with offers of horses. Then came a period in Herr Freitag's stables. In the meantime, I went back home and after that, back to Herr Freitag's again. Then my father died and finally I returned to Mühlen. By now it had become known that I could do things with horses. My training methods, which were different from those of other riders, were usually accepted. And all this happened because I had been a one day wonder in Munich which, in turn was due to a night on the tiles, wearing my best black suit!"

Rome 1960

Show jumpers – dressage riders even more – don't spring up ready made overnight. There are no surprises at the big championships. The winners are recruited from those dozen riders who have been known about for years. There have been cases where the young and inexperienced have been named as favourites – Gerd Wiltfang, for instance, at the Munich Olympic Games – but they are soon put in their place by the ruthlessness of the big arena, and sent back to finish their apprenticeship. At first, they may not be aware of the sudden pressure, but no one is sufficiently hardboiled to shake it off entirely. One may have won a stack of big prizes against the stiffest competition, but on these occasions there is only a sense of liberation, a feeling that one is riding for oneself. With all the emphasis today on the importance of the ego, it may sound slightly ridiculous to suggest that there are occasions when one is riding "for one's country".

Five years after his Munich adventure, Alwin Schockemöhle became one of the Olympic champions who rode for Germany in the team event with Fritz Thiedemann and Hans Günter Winkler. There had been an objection from the riders of the then Soviet Zone, which he had successfully resisted. In the individual event at the Games, which took place in the beautiful stadium of the Piazza di Siena in Rome, Ferdl, ridden by Schockemöhle collected penalty after penalty in the first round. He even fell and that meant 35·75 faults in all. In the second round, things went more smoothly with only 12·25 faults. He was placed 26th out of 60 starters.

In the Nations' Cup which concluded the games, there were rave notices about the German horses, who were said to have "the highest degree of agility", most of all Schockemöhle's Ferdl. Here it should be borne in mind

19

that Winkler was riding Halla, and Thiedemann was on Meteor. The same writer reported as follows on Schockemöhle's rounds for the Nations' Cup – (*Thiedemann on Meteor 17·75 faults, Winkler on Halla 13·75*):

"Wiser after his experiences in the previous individual event, Schockemöhle rides Ferdl with the utmost concentration and impressive calm, strongly gathering his horse before each jump and then taking off with extraordinary impulsion, so that his excellent synchronisation allows the horse to soar through the air. There was one mistake at the water jump and another at the first element on the double combination. For slightly exceeding the time allowance, he receives a half fault. In the second round, he is more attentive still. It is very noticeable that the rider is concentrating on avoiding faults at a risk of incurring time penalties. On this occasion, too, the gelding collects a fault at the water jump. Ferdl makes another slip at the final jump, catching his hoof on a pole of the oxer. Again there is a minor time fault and the scoreboard registers 8·75 – a total of 17·75 for the two rounds. 'Good old Schockemöhle! Well done!' says the applause, which comes particularly from the German spectators' block. Even if no one actually saw it, the rider must surely have sighed with relief, and that is something one can well understand."

So much for the contemporary observer. It doesn't seem so long ago, yet this passage might also be studied as an example of the change in the style of reporting.

Alwin Schockemöhle:

"Of course it was a great experience to ride in a team with my heroes and to manage to win. But for me they had long ceased to be inaccessible gods. I had come closer to them – indeed I had already beaten them. The period in which I was really proud of my achievements, when I felt delighted every time I went one better than the great ones, was much earlier – in the second half of the fifties. I had won the Jumping Derby in Hamburg by then, over the most difficult course in the world. I had been second in the Aachen Grand Prix – I had already arrived. My heroes of yesterday had already accepted me for some time past as a rival to be taken seriously."

At some time or other, there is the casual remark: "And

then I took over the family property." It sounds so natural, like saying: "And then it started raining." A young man, just turned twenty, undertakes responsibility for a fair-sized estate. There is no doubt that he has a well developed business flair – this he has proved ever since there were horses at his disposal, ever since he has known how to buy horses cheap and sell them again at a profit. Here is a young man who has saved money – let's say something like 100,000 D-marks, a tremendous sum in those days at the end of the fifties and the beginning of the sixties. Even nowadays it's a tidy amount. It was more than other young men possessed – but he had worked harder, much harder, than others. Is there a law against being a capable businessman?

And there is also the family estate which, as already mentioned, has been in their hands for 400 years. It is more than mere ownership or capital. It is hard for the city dweller in a rented flat to understand its true significance. When a young man reaches twenty, say, he acts more by feel or instinct than by pure reason. This particular young man had a fair amount of money, which he invested in an estate then very much in debt.

Alwin Schockemöhle:

"There were really no problems on that score. Apart from my sister, who is older, the others were still children. They can't have known what was going on at the time. They went to school as usual, and I saw to the farm. Of course I still kept horses, I took part in many horse shows and I had my successes. These wins really happened before the others got up in the morning, and in the evening – very late in the evening, actually, because it was only then I could find time for working with the horses. Later on, I found a partner to share this side of my activities. He is Otto Schulte-Frohlinde, and we have become friends. We owned the horses jointly, which helped me considerably. Obviously, it halved the risk. But at the beginning I had to carry the financial risk alone. There was no wealthy patron around offering me his stables. I had no financial backing – I had nothing. I bought my first horses, or else I borrowed them. Then I sold them. It was damnably hard, sometimes."

Anaconda and Rex the Robber

In equestrian sport, there are two closely connected themes which are vital to it and which often give rise to controversy. The first of these is the question put by the animal lover, trying to probe the relationship between rider and mount. There are innumerable heart-rending stories where the feelings involved are even described as "friendship" – like the special bond that exists between some people and their cat or dog. The pet cemetery in Hollywood is only an extreme caricature of such an expression of love of animals. Does it exist between riders and horses? Here, no doubt, it is important to differentiate between one hundred per cent sporting riders, and those who keep a horse as many others keep a dog.

Is there such a relationship, or is the horse merely an object essential to the sport – in the same category as a football or a bicycle? This brings us to the second point under discussion. Are riders really to be classed as amateurs, as laid down in the Olympic rules? Can a man be an amateur if he buys a horse for, say, 30,000 D-marks, wins races with it, and then sells it again for, say, 100,000 D-marks?

The story of Hans Günter Winkler's career has almost been forgotten, it happened so long ago. After the war, Winkler worked for a few years with the Allied occupation forces as a riding instructor. Because of this, a move was actually started to prevent him from taking part in the Olympics – although after a while, the whole thing was quietly dropped.

Another instance is that of the Swedish gold medallist in the three-day event, whose name was Kastenmann. In 1956, he was given a nominal promotion to the rank of officer for the period of the games, since a mere N.C.O. was not allowed to enter. This was because no one would credit a person from the lower echelons of the service with really being an amateur. After winning the gold, Kastenmann was demoted and returned to the ranks.

Or there is the more recent example of the British riders who have been classed as professionals as a body. Harvey Smith, a blunt Yorkshireman and a friend of Alwin Schockemöhle's, has no objection to being suddenly classed officially as a professional rider. He hoots with laughter at the so-called amateur status of many of his competitors.

Alwin Schockemöhle:

"I don't know if everything I did in the old days was always strictly in accordance with amateur regulations. But I can safely say that it is certainly the case today. If you like, today I can afford to be an amateur. At that time, if someone offered me a large sum of money, it wouldn't have been fair to my business to have hung on to the horse – I was compelled to sell it, even if I regretted doing so, even when I would have preferred not to. I had to do it to keep up my riding stables. If I had been forbidden to do so because of some rule or other, I'm sure there wouldn't have been an Alwin Schockemöhle in show jumping today.

"Take Anaconda, for example. This grey mare was not only good, she was a real beauty into the bargain. She was one of my first 'discoveries' and I had trained her personally. She had been up for auction because her owner couldn't manage her very well – and she wasn't very good at jumping either. In a relatively short time she learned a great deal at my hands. I entered her for international competitions and she won. All at once a number of people were interested in the horse and I was offered substantial amounts of money for her. I could have done with the cash but I liked the mare and I wanted to keep her. I've always liked greys, although colour isn't really any indication of class in a horse.

"And then Mary Mairs, who later married Frank Chapot, arrived from the United States. Later they both took part in the Olympic Games. Once Mary set eyes on Anaconda, she wouldn't leave me alone. If people say I forced the price up, it simply isn't true. A few days later, Mary produced a cheque for $25,000 from her pocket. Twentyfive thousand dollars – with the dollar standing at four D-marks then. It was a fantastic price. I don't believe so much had ever before been offered for a show jumper.

"It's different today, but there I was. I simply couldn't afford to refuse an offer like that. When I look back, I remember being a bit angry with Mary. However, the horse went to the United States. Much has been written about this, and even more has been said about it, but what ought I to have done? Should I have turned up my nose at the offer and refused? Horses aren't a particularly reliable capital investment. What would have happened if Anaconda had fallen sick a few days later, if she'd stopped jumping well, or if she had died? Then the same critics would probably have said: 'What a fool! Why didn't he sell?' In the circumstances it would have been irresponsible and selfish to have kept the mare for myself. But believe me, it was a hard decision. And I took it very reluctantly.

"Anaconda was beautiful and with me she would very likely have become a super horse. I have never changed that opinion. She was just six years old when I entered her at Aachen. She didn't make a single slip at any of the jumps, and it was a particularly difficult course. I mean it when I say that her loss really hurt me, in spite of all the dollars I got for her.

"One mustn't over or undervalue a rider's feelings for his horse. There are an awful lot of stories which credit animals to some extent with human characteristics. There are weird exponents of this doctrine who saw Halla laugh and Meteor grin, and goodness knows what besides. And in fiction, in boys' adventure stories, for instance, a rider whispers a word in his horse's ear, whereupon the animal immediately performs some wholly incredible feat. I'm very sceptical about this. No matter how sympathetic you are, you must never let yourself be carried away.

"Nowadays I'm in a different position vis-à-vis horse ownership. Today if Frank Chapot or his wife Mary waved a $100,000 cheque at me for one of my top horses like Warwick or Rex the Robber, I'd send them packing. I've become independent, financially and businesswise. I can afford to keep these horses – even if I'm suddenly offered that kind of money. If you like, it's one of the

24

advantages I've worked for all these years, something that makes me go on working even today. The independence which my money gives me is the most enjoyable thing about it. Naturally, it's all linked up with my love of riding as such, and also with competing at the Olympic Games and other big championships. I know that I can win with horses like these, and who doesn't like winning? There are riders who believe they need only buy the right horse and they're half way towards winning a gold medal. It's all right for them – but it wouldn't do for me.

"If a horse suits me, I try to keep it. I no longer need to sell it in order to make money from the sale. Very often I have a number of young horses in the stables. Sometimes I may buy a few, young or old, and then sell them again, because I can tell that they're not right for me personally. Horses like that might very well be fine in someone else's hands, but I can't shed tears over them. I know that they would never be winners with me.

"Of course there are horses you get particularly fond of and these I keep, although I've often had reason to wish them anywhere else but in my stables. Some kind of emotion is involved but it's completely one-sided and exists only from the human point of view. Love, I'd say, is much too strong a word. Affection is better. Rex the Robber means much more to me than Warwick, for instance. Robber is extremely sensitive and, if such a thing is possible in a horse, I'd call him more intelligent. I nickname him the Professor. Everyone knows that Robber is unreliable, that he has disappointed me, that I've made some wonderful bellyflops with him, but I'd never part with him. It would be much harder to say goodbye to him than to Warwick. One day, when Rex the Robber can't jump any more, I'll ride him just for pleasure and feed him and enjoy being with him. Maybe it's a special kind of sentimentality, even a bit crazy, but there it is.

"I know that when one talks of a horse's intelligence, it can't really be substantiated, scientifically speaking. What is certain is that some horses are more sensitive than others, that they respond much more to external influences. If it didn't sound too human, I'd call them good and bad tempered horses, the latter being more subject to moods than others. Robber is undoubtedly one of these. I love him with all his weaknesses as well as his strengths. I think he is quicker to grasp things than other horses. I also consider that his nickname, the Professor, is justified. But if other horses played me up as Robber does, I would soon get rid of them. Then again, there are horses that never give you any trouble, but who leave you cold. Rex the Robber is always on my mind. He takes all my attention, and he even keeps me awake at night. If I stop concentrating on him for a moment, he's liable to throw a tantrum. I often think how I could have done things differently – or better – with Robber; how I can get closer to him. Very likely the sheer difficulty of managing him is what fascinates me about him. He has created so many problems in such different areas that I can't live without them any more."

Career without Legends

Alwin Schockemöhle is about 5 feet 8 inches tall, broad shouldered, dark haired and with quick eyes. He seems to like taking risks but ones that can be calculated in advance. He is certainly no dreamer, nor a folk hero as Fritz Thiedemann was. One can feel fairly sure there will never be any legends built round him, as with Halla and Hans Günter Winkler, when he won the Stockholm gold medal in 1956. Furthermore, Schockemöhle's name is never associated with a single horse, as was the case with the other two, who became famous at a time when there weren't so many German names among the champions as there are today.

Schockemöhle is associated with a stableful of horses. One may begin with Ferdl, the horse he rode at the Rome Olympics. Then there was Freiherr who four years later, after very many successes, had to go and let him down at the Tokyo Olympic Games, of all places. There are also the fast horses Pesgö, the tremendously strong Winzer, Bacchus, Athlet, Wimpel, Donald Rex, Rex the Robber and, more recently, Warwick Rex. The list is surely not complete yet. Especially in the early stages of his career, Schockemöhle was often reproached for using training methods tailormade for himself only; no one else rides that way, "hunched", yet taut as a bowstring; no one else creates so strong an image of the horse in complete subordination. No other rider seems so to dominate his mount. He gives the impression that he could force the horse over the obstacle by sheer strength.

The notion that Alwin Schockemöhle's horses can only be ridden by him has long since proved to be mistaken. A striking example was in the exchange of horses event in the 1970 World Championship, when Donald Rex became top horse. Even when ridden by the other finalists, this gelding performed superlatively and under-lined the correctness of Schockemöhle's training methods. His system is justified not only in the so called "speed" tests, but also when a jump-off is required, as in the puissance trials.

He loves big horses. He must have an instinctive eye for their suitability. Probably he looks for horses which correspond to his personal taste; experts speak of their well muscled hindquarters, of an imposing outline, of strong galloping capacity, of a long croup, and a long but firm back. His way of riding is hard on his own back, and this will be referred to later. One would scarcely re-commend other riders to copy his methods. For the purists, he sits "too far back", which doesn't prevent other writers from praising his "laughing thighs" and "eloquent calves". He makes his horse "fly"; his seat is forever driving the horse on; immediately after the jump, the croup comes into play again; he never allows the horse's instinct to take the initiative. It is all definitely the result of several decades of hard work and equally lengthy discipline, plus an almost fanatical obsession with maintaining standards once they have been achieved.
Alwin Schockemöhle:
"My horses have all contributed their share to my career, whether they were called Ferdl, Freiherr or what-ever. But perhaps there is one I would like to single out and that is Donald Rex. He was an exceptional horse, probably the best in the world in his day. I have been riding in international events now for two decades and I think I know a bit about them. Many experts have backed me up in this opinion. Donald Rex has even been rated above Simona, Halla or Meteor by some people.

"Constitutionally, this gelding was not particularly strong or hardy, but no horse before or since was Donald Rex's equal in quality, in jumping capacity or response to all the aids one uses. There was nothing Donald Rex couldn't do, and in every single field he had the edge on all the others. And yet I never won any of the big championships titles with him. Perhaps it was my fault, perhaps it was his – who knows? In Mexico at the Olympics, he and I were the best pair in the Nations' Cup. If the regulations applying in Tokyo in 1964 had

28

been in force in Mexico, I'd have won the gold. But even if one can name Donald Rex in the same breath as other great show jumpers, he had one disadvantage. His career competing in the big championships was relatively short. I had only about two years all told with Donald Rex.

"During this period I won many major prizes and jumping trials. At the European Championships event in England, Donald Rex was second, although David Broome and I had the same number of points. Looking back on it, one might perhaps mention that the obstacles there were more to the taste of the English riders than the German. With Donald Rex I once won fifteen major awards in a row, and that, I believe, is a feat no other horse has ever accomplished with only two years in the field.

"At the Regen trials in Aachen in 1971, a year before the Munich Olympics, Donald Rex was injured. I had to arrange for him to have an operation on his back and, in retrospect, it must be admitted that it was not a success. He has been put out to grass at Otto Schulte-Frohlinde's place and he sometimes exercises Donald. Whenever I see him there, I think: 'What a pity!' He was a great horse, whose career reached its peak at a time when things weren't really right for him. He deserved much better."

And so, in years to come, when the great riding legends are being recorded, the reader will look in vain for the name of one particular horse to associate with Alwin Schockemöhle. This opens up the question of who deserves the greater credit, the horse or the rider. With show jumping, as opposed to horse racing, there is one noteworthy difference. In jumping, the rider is always named, no matter which horse he is riding. In racing, it is always the horse, with far less stress on the jockey's role. The explanation for this is relatively straight-forward.

Alwin Schockemöhle:
"In the really great triumphs, the rider must be as precisely on form as the horse. One cannot do without the other. Of course the degree of difficulty of the course also plays a decisive role here too. There are ordinary courses where a first class horse can win with only a moderately good rider. But with a really testing course, this can't happen.

29

"The story of Hans Günter Winkler and Halla seems at first glance to contradict this. Winkler was badly hurt and could hardly do anything to help and yet he won. Such occasions give rise to those moving stories about comradeship – 'faithful unto death' and all that nonesense. I was not in Stockholm at the time, but over the years I've learned enough of the game to allow myself to give a considered opinion. It simply doesn't make sense to say that Halla here, as the saying goes, carried her rider to victory all by herself. People who say that clean forget that Winkler had worked with this mare for years past. He and no one else had made her into the kind of showjumper she had become. There is, deep down, a kind of mutal trust. Winkler, in spite of being in pain, knew from experience what the horse would do. And she, in turn, felt the rider's presence and did instinctively what the rider wanted, even without being made to. This ride was proof of his careful schooling over a long period of time. To put it in a nutshell: I believe that Halla would have completed two more virtually fault-free rounds carrying the almost helpless Winkler – but then she would have had to stop. Perhaps one can explain it with an example from business life. A bank or a big concern also carries on for a while when the boss is absent. Then a decision must be made, which is all important for the success or failure of the firm. At that point, he is needed personally and no one else will do.

"In my view, the situation in Stockholm was comparable. Halla was attuned to an outstanding rider – but only to him, to Hans Günter Winkler, on that particular day. Probably she had something one might call confidence in him. She was aware that she must jump over an obstacle at a certain point to which the rider was directing her. That's all it was. From what I know, and I keep coming back to this, it's the only possible explanation. At that moment, all Winkler's previous training paid off handsomely. Another rider at that moment couldn't have been certain of even completing the round, unless he had worked with the horse previously. Halla was an exceptional horse, and Winkler an exceptional rider.

"If a rider such as Raimondo d'Inzeo had had the mare under training for a long time, a similar result might have been possible, but who can say? It's all speculation. Today I can judge the situation more coolly, although at the time it happened I too believed that there must have been a special secret relationship."

Looking for Horses

The qualities of a rider, are therefore, of great importance, but it is essential, to achieve success, to choose the right type of horse. The class of a horse is subject to development over many years of training, but if the quality is not there in the beginning even the best trainer can not achieve much. Therefore any top rider is constantly on the look out for new horses for his stable, and for new possibilities which can bring him success in the future.

There are many well known examples of this. The West German rider Herman Schridde is one of the most talented riders in the world, but for years now he has had no horses, and consequently one hears nothing about him. The great secret of Alwin Schockemöhle is that he is a combination of rider and horsetrader. Just like his colleagues Alwin is constantly searching for new horses. His stables at Mühlen are a transit camp for scores of horses and he is in daily contact with colleagues in the horse trading business; the telephone at his house rings constantly.

Alwin Schockemöhle:

"I believe there is hardly any other country in the world where there is so much constant contact between horse people, especially in this part of West Germany. Hardly an hour passes without somebody telephoning me; not only from inside Germany but also from abroad I hear about the newest developments. A rider like Johan Heins regularly telephones me. My horse The Robber is at present resting in David Broome's stables, so I am in regular communication with him too. There are only very few really top horses and every top class rider is looking out for them. It is quite obvious therefore that one has to be very keen eyed and quick to get hold of such a treasure. I have had, over the years, a few top

Looking ahead . . .

. . . reached its peak in
Mexico, 1972

"I've always liked greys!"

European Champion twice over – Alwin Schockemöhle on Warwick Rex, winner of the individual event and also a member of the winning German team. Seen here with the other team members Hendrik Snoek, Sönke Sönksen and Hartwig Steenken Munich 1975

Santa Monica

Perspectives

Rex the Robber, nicknamed
the "Professor," his
favourite

class horses, but not many; some of them are: Freiherr, Freya, Donald Rex, Warwick Rex, Rex the Robber. Add to this that horses like Rex the Robber are not right for every occasion; for example he is much too careful for an Olympic course. When things become really difficult he sometimes gets confused because he is so cautious and the result then is a series of refusals.

"Warwick does not have this hesitance. He has an enormous jumping potential but does not worry overmuch if he makes a little mistake now and then. He just takes the next obstacle undisturbed. Such a horse, with great jumping qualities and unflappability is the ideal Olympic horse. I knew that before the Olympics; that is why we did everything possible to get Warwick fit and ready for the start. We knew we would stand a good chance of winning if we could get him fit. The great winners in past history often possessed the same qualities: this combination of jumping quality and character. If, measuring them by this standard, one had to choose the top horses in West Germany, then I would only name Halla, Meteor, Donald, Simona and Warwick. Such horses you don't just pick up every day, they only appear once or twice in a generation. When you buy a horse you can never be sure whether he does have this absolute top class. That will have to be discovered in using him. There are horses which can easily jump 2 metres (6ft 6ins) but which will not be able to complete a 1·50 metres (4ft 11ins) course without faults".

Alwin Schockemöhle has bought horses during his career of which he had the highest hopes and which disappointed him thoroughly. The opposite, however, has also happened: his Olympic horse Warwick Rex, he bought from the horsedealer Friedrich Ernst in Verden, while everyone else had already written him off for top sport. Yet with this horse Alwin gained the first two international titles of his career, The European and Olympic championships. One can therefore see that luck does play a certain part in finding really top quality horses. You can assist luck by great expertise and by buying and trying out as many top horses as possible.

Alwin Schockemöhle:

"When I go to look over a horse, I of course look for certain characteristics. First, a horse must be able to jump, that is he must have the power to jump high. Often I detect this quality already when he jumps an obstacle of 1·20 or 1·30 metres (3ft 11ins to 4ft 2ins). There are of course horses which do not impress me jumping at this height but which get better the higher they are requested to jump. In young horses it is important that they possess the courage to take off early when they jump. If they take off very early, yet have no problem getting over the obstacle, you can practically be certain they have class.

"A second important point is the technique of a horse, that is the way he folds his legs under his body and the speed with which he does it. It is important for a horse to be very quick with his foreleg and to be able to fold it under him in a fraction of a second when necessary. Yet there are horses with little ideal technique which still belong to the top class. For example Warwick Rex has so much talent that he does not have to take any trouble over lower obstacles. He doesn't fold his legs quickly, he lets them trail. Yet when he has to jump high obstacles or when he is in a tight take off situation he suddenly *does* have the necessary technique. A third point that I find very important is good balance. The neck of a horse is his balance mechanism; he regulates his equilibrium with his neck. A horse has to throw his neck forwards and downwards when taking an obstacle; he must round his body to a half circle, when jumping. There are indeed some successful horses which do not do this, but I prefer a horse with good balance. Sometimes one thinks that it depends on the rider whether a horse is balanced or not; for example Ann Moore's horses always jumped with straight necks and without using their backs.

"Actually English riders often ride horses that do not balance perfectly. On the other hand Simona and Donald Rex balance perfectly. Donald was a horse with ideal behaviour patterns over obstacles, a pleasure for rider and spectator alike. During my career I have only had one horse that did not balance perfectly and that was Santa Monica. That was a horse I bought from a Dutch rider Van Cruchten and I sold it later to a Canadian. Everyone thought that Santa Monica was a horse that was easy to ride, but this was not so. Because of her imperfect balance, this mare was much more difficult than anyone thought.

To get this horse correctly over an obstacle was difficult, it required real riding skills. Therefore I avoid horses that lack balance because it interferes with my style. Apart from the three points indicated above, there are other things I take into account when buying a horse; for example whether a horse is good in the mouth. That you can only tell after riding it and even then this sometimes changes during later use. In my experience I have found however, that a sound mouth like a good balance more often than not is inborn. Training can make a difference but the better the material the better the result.

"When buying a horse the one most important point is character. If a horse has no character it is suspect – leave it alone! If I see a shifty nervous unco-ordinated horse then I do not need to see it saddled, I already know! For this reason I prefer Hanoverians, good of character, steady and they suit me."

Apart from the qualities which Alwin Schockemöhle named and which he bears in mind when he buys horses, there are of course countless other factors which he takes into consideration when making a judgement. As a good horseman he is fantastically quick in analysing the physique of a horse. He sees at once whether its four legs are healthy, whether its body is sinewy enough and well proportioned, whether it has a friendly eye and many more characteristics.

Alwin Schockemöhle also bears in mind that he is searching for a horse that suits him personally. The horse he is looking for must suit his methods, and let itself be ridden in the typical Schockemöhle fashion. His dominant style, and his deep seat demand a rather heavy horse with not too fiery a character. Other horses suit other riders better. Often one finds, according to Alwin Schockemöhle, that the style of riding adopted by riders of a specific country is dependent on the particular kind of horse that is bred in that country.

"If I had been born in America and therefore had ridden Thoroughbreds from youth my style would have developed quite differently. Our German horses are heavies and need more control, the result is our style of riding is different."

Apart from all this there is still a most important factor in the choice of the ideal jumper:

Alwin Schockemöhle:

"The family tree has become more and more important. Through practice we have discovered that some families of mares and stallions produce more good jumpers than others. This cannot always be detected from observing them from outside. Jumpers can originate from the most unexpected corners. Don't be surprised if one day you find yourself in the small dark stable of an Oldenburg peasant and his carthorse. Gold often is hidden deep, and it is not to be found in the colour of skin and flesh; it is to be found inside the rib cage. I often get sent thin and skinny horses, but I buy them because I see them take *one* correct step. A feeling for horses is innate, but be sure not to let this hunch have too much of a say; the background of a horse tells you just as much. There are some famous sires which really do not *look* much: for example Pick Ash and Der Lowe are only middling horses, and Furioso was no wonder horse either. That is what makes it so complicated – which norms should one take? Appearance and performance do not mean everything; temper, health and solidity mean at least as much. Choosing and buying the right horses is a complicated matter. It is a combination of feeling, knowledge and luck.

"Only someone who lives in the world of equestrian sport and who grew up among horses can ever hope and expect to find, now and then, a horse of world class. At least if he, as I am prepared to, is ready to search day in day out, to look at hundreds of horses a year and to buy and try out dozens of them. Only then is one not totally dependent on luck to find a top horse, although luck will always play a rôle. Perhaps that is what makes this sport so fascinating."

Style and Pain

Prominent sportsmen are exceptionally good models for young people. They are at an age when physical skills play an important rôle in life. This is one reason. Another lies in the fact that, when you stop to think about it, sport – or at least competitive sport – is basically an old-fashioned activity. It is oldfashioned in the sense that in modern times, as opposed to the age of the hunter, it is no longer necessary for survival to be able to run fast, aim accurately, wrestle or box effectively, or to throw far. The man who used to have to hurl a spear in order to make sure of his dinner, nowadays sits at the conference table drinking coffee, or stands behind a shop counter.

Alwin Schockemöhle:

"I've no objection if boys today say that I am their idol. At first, a boy admires his father. Then he looks elsewhere for his heroes. When my life became more and more concerned with horses, I too had my heroes, of course. But here one must make a distinction. One person was to be admired, but one tried to model oneself on someone else. As a boy, I admired Winkler and Thiedemann, but I wanted to be able to ride like Raimondo d'Inzeo. In one respect that still holds good today. My feelings when I watch him ride are quite different from those I have towards other horsemen.

"I have been tremendously influenced by the Italian master, not only in the arena, but most of all in schooling and training. Naturally I have also adopted various details from other riders and adapted them for my own purposes, but most of them come from Raimondo d'Inzeo. However, the decisive factor was that I didn't confine myself to observing him at competitions. A rider's real work takes place at home – and this is probably true for much more than riding. At horse shows, only the result of your labour is visible, and not how your success was arrived at. But that is the really interesting and useful part of it.

"And then one day the truth dawns on you that you can't simply adopt something blindly – because it won't fit in with other things, and because what is good for one person isn't necessarily right for another, not by a long chalk. There exists a certain class, a certain standard. After that, you must put it all together for yourself and establish a style of your own. Style – all it means is putting your personal stamp on all you have learnt.

"Riders in specific countries often have adopted their style to the kind of horse that is available. Our heavy halfbreeds need a lot of control, that is why West German riders usually do everything themselves. Their style is much more dominant than, for example, the style of the Americans, who often ride Thoroughbreds. If I had grown up in America, my style would be completely different."

There are some riders who try to mould all their horses into one system, while others always try as riders to adapt themselves to the horse they ride. Alwin Schockemöhle belongs to the first category; he always rides in the same fashion whether he rides the Anglo-Arab, Rex the Robber, or the heavy Hanoverian Warwick. He subjects all his horses to the same principle and to the same system.

Alwin Schockemöhle:
"A man like Harvey Smith goes from one extreme to the other. One day he will be riding a horse with a double bridle, the next day he suddenly uses a totally different bit. There is no system. I try to work as much as possible in one particular way. For years I have only used an ordinary bridoon; only when riding Warwick do I need a gag. The difference between Harvey and myself is enormous. I have to bend a horse completely to my will; I must thoroughly train it and make it obey me before I will bring him out. Harvey does not need so much time; he even takes bad horses with him to competitions, and what is more he even wins with them!

"That is because physically he is so strong, he can bend a horse shoe with his bare hands. He can do things that others cannot. Which is not to say that he only uses

54

force, for his best horses often go very lightly; but still force takes an important place in Harvey's style of riding. Style depends a lot on the build of the rider. All top riders are built differently, therefore all their styles differ."

Alwin Schockemöhle has been a good observer all his life. He spent hundreds of hours observing top riders during their training sessions and during competitions. From this observation of others he has built his own system. It is therefore interesting to hear what he thinks of his most important colleagues.

Alwin Schockemöhle:

"Raimondo d'Inzeo is the best rider in the world. I want to get where he is. With him everything is of the highest standard. In dressage, his horses have style; it is pure joy to observe them; he controls them beautifully, and they win competitions. But there is one drawback: for years he has not had enough horses and so he has been forced to make them perform too much. That is why he rode old Bellevue for so long even when he had to be kept upright by artificial means.

"I especially admire in him his elegance achieved by adapting his concentration and harmony to that of the horse. With his brother Piero d'Inzeo, style often takes precedence over effectiveness and Piero's horses often throw their heads high before taking an obstacle. He never corrects them and that is why his horses often make unnecessary mistakes. Over the years Raimondo has always been better than Piero in the big competitions.

"After Raimondo I think that Nelson Pessoa and Caroline Bradley are very good, at the moment. Nelson's first generation of horses developed without any trouble and he did it all his way. That was the time of Huipil and Gran Geste. Lately he has had to work hard with his young horses. With Nelson and Caroline it looks as if the horses arrive completely naturally at the correct point of take-off before an obstacle.

"Of course they ride with the same control as I demand from my horses but with them it all flows so well! The whole trick is to bring the horse at the right speed to the correct point of take-off. The speed varies with different obstacles. At a width jump one has to have a higher speed than at a height jump. Riders with West German Style, like me, often make sharper commands to change their

1

My style could be much more elegant, but I have been riding by myself the last few years. If there had been somebody to point out my mistakes then my style would perhaps have improved. There are all kinds of little mistakes which have no influence upon the final performances but which are not so attractive when you look at a series of photographs

2

The first two photographs were taken of me riding Warwick Rex towards an obstacle during the international horse trials in Rotterdam. In the second photograph, I obviously have the measure of it; it is clearly a width jump, because I'm riding quite fiercely towards it and I am giving the horse every freedom to jump from a gallop. If it had been a difficult height jump, I certainly would have kept him on a shorter rein

3

Here you see the beginning of the take-off. The hindlegs are well under at the point of take-off, and the forequarters are already on the upward. I have brought my hands back because I wanted to keep contact with his mouth during take off. You can already see that his hindquarters are going to be in exactly the right position

4

The take-off. Within a fraction of a second the horse will leave the ground. He is therefore at the beginning of the climbing phase of the jump; technically all is correct. Notice that my hand gives complete freedom to the horse so that he can balance his neck to bring himself into correct equilibrium

5

This is an interesting photograph. The horse is nicely rounded. Postures of rider and horse are exemplary. It can be seen here how Warwick Rex does not fold his front legs completely. He has so much power that he takes this hurdle easily without having to strain himself. Just as in the previous photograph, my hand is loose, and I am even giving him a little too much rein. During training I normally ride with a loose rein and the pull required is nearly twice as much as with a tight rein. Consequently I do tend to use too much rein when I should be riding a course on a tighter one

6

After the first phase of the jump, the climb and the flight above the obstacle, the landing begins. Warwick begins to fold his front legs; he brings his nose forward and I myself move back into the saddle a little

56

7

Just before the landing. Not a good photograph as far as my riding technique is concerned. I am just too far back in the saddle and I am supporting myself with my knees, while I really should find support in the stirrups; yet the horse, as you can see, is not adversely affected. These are aesthetic faults

8

The landing itself. Notice that all the weight is completely on the left foreleg. Now you can understand what strain these legs suffer if one is not careful. My posture is quite good, even if it looks as though I am trying to support my hands on the neck of the horse

9

The first gallop jump. I have leaned forward and am giving the horse a chance to stretch himself. After this I will begin to collect him. The horse has to be brought back on to his hindquarters. You can see that at this point of the jump the weight is still too much on the forequarters

speed or to prepare for take-off".

About four times a year the various styles of the best riders in the world are tested in the World Championship. The four best combinations then ride each other's horses in the final. The rider with the least faults becomes World Champion. Although it has its opponents, this formula is still very interesting. It makes it possible to see how certain riders can adopt themselves to completely strange horses. One then sees a real confrontation of styles. A beautifully trained horse, which gets rough riders will almost certainly protest and resist. A fine rider on a rough horse will have his hands full to make the horse perform to his wishes. It is therefore not all that remarkable that over the last few years the world title was not won by riders who display one obvious developed style, but by riders who can adapt themselves quickly to changed circumstances and who are used to riding different horses.

That is why Hartwig Steenken won at Hickstead, while the most stylish rider of this event was without doubt the young Irish rider Eddie Macken.

Also a rider like Alwin Schockemöhle is at a disadvantage in such a final. Four years previous to Hickstead, at La Baule in France, he was the great favourite with his horse Donald Rex. Why did he not succeed then in obtaining the title?

Alwin Schockemöhle:

"David Broome won the title on that occasion. He undoubtedly was at that moment the best in the transferred horses event. He can ride any kind of horse and he makes the best of the worst. You don't need excuses when you do not win the World Championship; there were at least ten possible candidates at La Baule, for example: Pesson, Winkler, Steinkraus, Chapot, d'Inzeo; and all of them lost.

"I did not enjoy the final riding David Broome's horse Beethoven. I have myself produced bad animals now and again, but that can't be the aim; I have quite different ideas about a champion horse. It doesn't please me to have to keep on shouting – 'steady,' 'steady.' If you give him a little you never get control again. Horses belonging to Pesson and Steinkraus have given me a lot more pleasure in the final. Hatty Brown, Harvey Smith's horse felt quite good at that time. He does ride dressage, so you can let his horses parade yet keep them under control. Everyone could ride my horse Donald Rex quite well at La Baule; it gave me a lot of pleasure because everyone could now see that my style of riding is not so different from that of others as people thought at that time". Alwin therefore obviously lost out because of his own good training.

The others rode excellent rounds on the well trained Donald Rex, while Alwin found it difficult to ride some of his competitors' horses well.

Riders who work according to a system are at a disadvantage in the final of the world championship. This is the objection that Alwin Schockemöhle has against such an event. Not the best combination but the cleverest rider wins the title.

Good Luck and Bad

What is good or bad luck? When Alwin Schockemöhle won the gold medal at the 1960 Olympics, all heaven was at his feet. A brilliant future? Yet four years later, at the Tokyo Games in 1964, he was a spectator in the stands. His horse was injured, and another competitor whose horse was also hurt had first claim on the reserve mount. In 1968 in Mexico, when Hermann Schridde's horse went to pieces, Alwin Schockemöhle was deprived of the chance of being once again a member of the winning team. But at least it could be said that it was only through his performance that the Germans won the bronze medal. At the Munich Olympics, 1972, he withdrew his entry before a decisive stage was reached – his best horses were sick and injured. At the World Championship he obtained good places, but victory eluded him. He took part in the European Championship ten times, and at last, on the tenth occasion, he won in Munich in 1975.

The ovation he was given by the spectators was not only for his achievement on the day, but also for himself as a man of whom it had been said so casually and so often in sporting circles: "It was long overdue." And the applause was, in addition, a tribute to a man who, it was known, is in pain almost every minute of his life. The first attack was at a ridiculously easy practice jump at a meeting in Neumünster. It happened again at La Baule in France, and then in Rome. There followed massage, physiotherapy, baths, visits to spas, plaster jackets, elastic bandages. But there was a series of victories in between, and he got used to wearing a surgical corset whenever he climbed into the saddle. "Fame or a wheelchair!" said one headline with the terrifyingly brutal frankness of which newspapers – and doctors too – are capable. No surgeon could guarantee

60

that any operation would remove the risk of the latter alternative. Schockemöhle once said that on those rare occasions when the pain recedes, he feels there's something missing.

Alwin Schockemöhle:

"I've always had trouble with my back. I know that the way I'm made, I have to sit differently in the saddle as compared with other riders. I should very much like to sit as far forward as Raimondo d'Inzeo. That would be my dream, but I can't.

"At first they called it sciatica, and that was that. Whoever takes any notice of a bit of pain like that, when one's young and feels as strong as a bull? That time in Neumünster I was in the collecting ring when something snapped and I was virtually unable to move. I fell off my horse and lay there like a limp rag. I couldn't even wriggle my toes – nothing. When this happens, you can't even think – you only feel the excruciating pain and hope it will soon stop. You can't even scream, although I may have groaned. I have the clearest memories of those moments. I shan't forget them to my dying day. I lay in the sawdust on the ground, and I could see the legs of the other riders' horses, as people came up to see what had happened to me. I remember their riding boots. And above them were faces. I can't remember who was there – just pale blobs of faces with dark, eyes, staring down at me.

"After that, I didn't ride again for six months. In all that time I didn't mount a horse – and that can only be appreciated if you know that since my childhood there wasn't a single day when I hadn't ridden at least once. During those six months I got worse and worse. The pain never eased off. Some doctors advised an immediate operation, others suggested other methods. Perhaps it would have been better if I'd forced myself to ride. During this long gap, the muscles in my back began to atrophy and as a result, the vertebrae had less support – at least that is how I as a layman understand the medical explanation. During this period it meant crawling on the floor to put on my shoes. But once I was riding again, I always felt better. Although the stabbing pain persisted, at least I felt I was capable of movement. My mind told me that it was actually the horse that was moving, but even so, it helped me to overcome my inner misgivings.

"I travelled across Europe from one doctor to another. I visited every specialist I was recommended. They all gave different opinions. I don't wish to blame any of them, because they all took a lot of trouble with me. The diagnosis that eventually emerged seems to be this: through the many spills I have had in the course of years, the ligaments have become stretched and as a result, the vertebrae keep slipping. And when this happens, it has the same effect as a slipped disc; that is, there is pressure on the nerve which causes pain – it's always the same spot, between the fourth and fifth vertebrae. It is possible to lock them into position by performing an operation, which involves removing bone from another part of the body and grafting it to reinforce the vertebrae. Then there would be no pain. But it's a risky operation, very risky.

"I had reached the point where I said: 'I've had enough. I'll have the operation.' And if they could guarantee its success, I'd pack my pyjamas and toothbrush tomorrow and go into hospital. But who can give such a guarantee? Time and again I've been told that in my case an operation would be a last resort, when I really can't move – when there's no alternative.

"So I only ride if I'm wearing a surgical corset. Otherwise, when I'm walking or standing, or making all the movements a normal person does in the course of twenty-four hours, I leave it off in order to strengthen the muscle system. Sometimes things are better, but only relatively speaking. I'm always in pain but I'm used to it. Nothing like the original experience has happened now for several years. I've never had another total collapse. Sometimes my walk is rather crooked and bent – but at least I can walk. And I ride a bit too!"

Until the 1975 European Championship, Alwin Schockemöhle was generally regarded as a "Champion without a Title". In fact, there is probably no sportsman in any field who had indisputably belonged to world class for such a long time, and who still had never won one of the major championships. Apart from complete physical fitness, which is essential for entering top grade competitions, there is one other factor for which training is hardly possible. Sportsmen and their coaches speak of "nerve", and this can mean many things. Nerve is, to a large extent, sheer cheek, a devil-may-care attitude, with even a suggestion of contempt for others. "Chutzpah", which the dictionary defines as "shameless audacity," is a very good word for it. At competitions, when it comes to two sportsmen of equal ability, the one with more "chutzpah" will always win. In a cool, unexcitable person like Alwin Schockemöhle, the absence of this characteristic comes as a surprise.

Take the European Championship of 1973, for instance, held at the Hickstead Trials in England, where he was the favourite at the start, and where his dreams came to an abrupt end at the water jump – formidable, admittedly, but nevertheless routine. On that occasion he blamed all and sundry for his failure, and it took some time before he admitted that he himself was to blame. This reaction suggests a very sensitive attitude. But after the fall, the burden of being the favourite was suddenly lifted from his shoulders. In the remaining events of the competition, the way Alwin Schockemöhle rode Rex the Robber was well ahead of his rivals, and it earned him admiring applause. In the end, he finished second – "only" second.

These experiences are very common. It is always happening – a kind of examination nerves, one might say. Without warning, one is seized by doubts about one's ability to win. The skier, Franz Klammer, used to put it this way: "Once you stop to think, you've already lost."
Alwin Schockemöhle:
"I don't want to gloss things over. I was often, too often, close to winning and yet I didn't pull it off. But I still believe that because of my equestrian schooling I'm as good as anyone else in the arena. There are a whole number of stronger riders – riders with more natural talent – but I think I can hold my own even with them. The experience I have acquired through the years comes into it. The fact that I tried so many times and still didn't win was due, in my opinion, to various reasons. I don't like using the terms, but good and bad luck do play a large rôle in sport. In fact, one should sometimes be glad of it. On three occasions I came second at major competitions on a total of points which previously would have been sufficient to have won. But one's personality plays a part too – one man or woman has better nerves, the other hasn't. You have to reconcile yourself to this. You

63

can't help it, any more than you can help having blue eyes. The only thing to do is to concentrate on more routine practice, but even increasing it day by day doesn't always help.

"To be sure there are riders with stronger nerves than mine. I can't alter that. It's something I have to live with. There are people who go home at night and they can switch themselves off like a radio set and sleep like a dormouse. I don't belong to that category. I get very worked up about what has happened sometimes. I think back and try to work out how I could have done something better, and how I shall tackle things next day. This goes on late into the night, and often enough it brings positive results, which the dormouse fails to achieve – because he doesn't reflect and he doesn't need to. You have to recognise your own shortcomings. Then they stop being disadvantages.

"I'm not unhappy about my 'not so strong' nerves, as many people call them. No one has ever said that they are actually weak. That would be utter nonsense. When you've been at this game for as long as I have – and, been successful at it – no one can accuse you of having weak nerves. I've won far too many really tough jumping contests over far too many years for anyone to say that. It's just that the competition has become much stronger. Years ago, let's say as many as twenty, there was just a handful of riders who shared the wins among themselves. Today, if you wanted to name the favourites for in-dividual events, you couldn't count them on the fingers of both hands.

"Vexations? Of course. I've had my share too. When people get ideas into their heads, they're sometimes hard to shift. For instance, people have held it against me that for many years Hans Günter Winkler reigned supreme – and still does, to some extent, even today. I believe one should look at the facts. For the last fifteen years almost, he and I have ridden against each other at all the com-petitions for the European Championship. Every time my placing has been better than his, but no one mentioned that. The reason is that by then I was the favourite, having won all the preceding events when he hadn't. But people kept writing and saying Schockemöhle had failed again –

Routine, according to Alwin Schockemöhle, is no more than weighing up the situation coolly and being prepared to take the right amount of risk. He had many successes in the mid 60's riding the gelding Exakt

64

Alwin Schockemöhle has mastered to perfection the art of coming to grips with the horse: swift collection, approach, canter and take-off are calculated to within a centimetre if possible. Here he is riding the famous Freiherr

Freiherr was a horse that seemed "made" for Alwin Schockemöhle. Until the mid 60's, he displayed a kind of "tense relaxation" which was the outcome of many years' work. At the time, it was said that no one else could ride his horses, a statement which has long since been refuted

In practice, Alwin Schockemöhle hardly ever allows the horse's instinct to take the initiative. The way he sits constantly urges the horse forward. Immediately after the jump, the croup comes into play again. (Here he is riding Romona)

"The fact that in Germany every good show jumping horse is given dressage schooling may well be looked on as one of the basic reasons why we have always been among the world's best riders." This photograph demonstrates very clearly, with Alwin Schockemöhle on the grey, Bacchus, actually making a jump, the rider's concentration at every stage. This is the whole secret of his success

he still hadn't managed to bring it off. Winkler wasn't mentioned at all in the same context – not even when he was placed well behind me. After all, on each occasion, we had both been sent there to win the title if possible, and not to indulge in a kind of private war.

"Don't misunderstand me though. Hans Winkler and I are certainly not what one would call the closest of friends, but we respect each other, we've ridden in the same team, we've won and we've lost together. That creates a bond – you can't be wholly indifferent to one another after that. But although Winkler was not, of course, responsible for the notices, they often rankled. When I started, Winkler was at the peak of his career. Today, for a variety of reasons, it has happened that I have usually had a string of major successes just before the Olympic Games or World or European Championships, and he hasn't. So they named me as the favourite, not him. It's often most unfair."

George Bernard Shaw once said that sport is an excellent means of making enemies of countries which otherwise have nothing at all against each other. There are many examples to confirm the truth of this cynical remark. Suddenly the Germans can't stand the Dutch, because one of their referees is alleged to have "picked" on a German football team. All at once, the Pakistanis abuse the Germans, because the latter won a hockey match. There are English riders who point a finger at everyone else, because they believe the others too are really professionals, as if to say: why should they get away with something when we're not allowed to?

Of course there are rules and there is also "fair play". Fair play is really no more than simply abiding by these rules. But it has nothing at all to do with friendship. Fair play is the natural courtesy of sportsmen. It is no more than an acknowledgment of the rule of law. Like courtesy, fair play requires perspective. It can also be very cool. But friendship is warm – it comes from the heart, even if one doesn't always display it.

Success and failure have one thing in common. They sift out ruthlessly the real from the so-called friendships. The people with most friends are those who steer a middle course and don't lean towards either extreme, either to the positive or the negative.

*...win Schockemöhle
...es big horses –
...scribed as having well-
...uscled hindquarters, an
...posing outline, the
...ility to canter power-
...lly, a long croup and a
...ng firm back. For
...nnoisseurs of style, Alwin
...hockemöhle sits too far
...ck. Even at Bromont
...ople argued about
...hether in fact he had
...dden "correctly".
...Here he is riding Exakt)*

Alwin Schockemöhle:

"In our sport there exists a problem which is almost unknown in any other – the problem of the generations. If you are good enough, you can go on riding for a long time, twenty or thirty years. The difference in age creates different interest groups, which is quite logical. With us there hardly exists what could be described as personal enmity. The reason is that during a competition we are not direct opponents. There's no such thing as physical confrontation as there is in boxing or in tennis for instance. Each man rides for himself, first and foremost against the obstacles, and secondly against the clock. The performances are recorded and then compared.

"But of course there are competitors with whom one gets on better than with others, simply as human beings. These people would probably also have made friends with each other if they had been in the habit of going to the same place for a drink, or happened to be in the same line of business. There are a number of riders with whom I get on particularly well, whose company I prefer to that of others. If that's friendship, O.K. Years ago I was closest to the riders I had grown up with, Hermann Schridde and Kurt Jarasinski. Today it's Hartwig Steenken. We telephone each other almost every day and talk about everything under the sun. This is an odd situation because we are actually the keenest rivals. Similarly with foreigners like David Broome or Nelson Pessoa. I get on with Broome better than I do with Graziano Mancinelli. That's how it is.

"Of course with most of the other competitors one just passes the time of day and that pretty well covers all we have in common. We all know that we need good horses to be able to win – to a large extent we're all aware of what the others have done by way of special preparation. I believe it isn't very different in other sports. One meets, the contest takes place, one congratulates or accepts congratulations, one says goodbye. We riders get together more frequently than most, because there are so many meetings. With minor exceptions, it's always the same gang.

"For at least fifteen years now I've been friends with David Broome, who's often beaten me, and just as often I've beaten him. I'd share everything with him. He's a real buddy. We don't need to say much to each other, but on the other hand we often chat for hours on end. It's as simple as that. He once said on British television that he wished he had a brother like me. When someone told me about it later, it gave me tremendous pleasure. Which other Englishman would have said – in England – that he would like to have a German for a brother?

"Of course one is most pleased when one wins oneself. But with David Broome, I'm just as pleased when he's ahead. He's a nice chap, someone I can always rely on one hundred per cent. I'd help him when he was in trouble, and it's good to know he'd do the same for me. These things are pretty rare.

"Mind you, I don't want to be misunderstood. It sounds very noble and all that nonsense. I didn't mean it that way. If you don't enter a competition dead keen to win, you might as well stay at home. This applies as much to riding as it does to any other sport. When I cross the starting line, all I think about is winning. Nothing else. This is probably the kind of ambition everybody needs – no matter what it is he's going in for. Whatever I undertake – in business as well – I want to be the best. Life is like that – my life at least. Anyone who believes things will fall into his lap ready made will have a long time to wait. Unfortunately such people are often the envious ones. They complain that Fate isn't kind to them, whereas they're just lazy.

"You must be able to drive yourself. When the others go for a drink at nine or ten in the evening, or slip away to watch a thriller on TV, then you have to stir your stumps and march off, left, right, into the practice ring, trying out the same jump over and over again for an hour or more. On Sundays and holidays too. There's no such thing as overtime if you want to achieve results in life.

"I'm always impressed by a good performance, no matter who gives it. When I know that a person has worked cleanly, that he's a good rider and a good horseman, it gives me great pleasure. But if I know that someone has won unfairly, I get very bitter. Such goings on are often exposed with a great deal of fuss – and rightly so. People like that not only get themselves into bad repute but the rest of us too. They know perfectly well that they've cheated – and they know too that we know. They count on us pretending to know nothing and saying nothing. And all at once, you find you're involved too. What should I do? Stand up and point them out? Ought I to say that what so-and-so is doing isn't fair? They put a strain on other people's efforts to play straight. They give nothing and only want to take. No – if I say sometimes I'll have nothing to do with certain people, I have my reasons. They must realise they're on their own, that they mustn't get others involved.

"To try to sum up: we horsemen are sometimes a bit different, even odd. If you like, we're all a bit crazy. But we're all enthusiastic about a beautiful horse. And if someone I've always considered weaker suddenly gives a fantastic performance and comes first, then it doesn't matter if I'm only fourth. I'm really and truly delighted.

"We all have certain ideals in our heads and we dream of seeing them fulfilled one day. You can't see yourself in that light. You always need to have someone else you can watch. That's what I mean."

Motivation

With Alwin Schockemöhle, there is little doubt that the framework of his life is just as important as his horses, his rise to fame and his riding successes. Certainly he has stronger family ties than he might admit in his rôle as a smart businessman. This has something to do with – among other things – his rural background, where people are more interdependent than in the anonymity of the city. Loneliness in the country is less than in the densely populated concentration of a town.

Alwin Schockemöhle's wife Gaby is pretty, blonde, petite and energetic and he met her first when she was still a child. She is the stepdaughter of one of his father's friends, with whom Alwin is still associated today. He is Otto Schulte-Frohlinde – nicknamed Schufro – and the two men became active partners, an efficient team working well together. They not only share the ownership of valuable horses but they have also tackled problems affecting the fundamentals of riding with a vigour and freshness seldom found in these circles.

Gabriele Wilshaus became Frau Alwin Schockemöhle and they went to live in Mühlen. Their children are Alexandra, Frank and Christoph.

Alwin Schockemöhle:

"I was often in Berlin in those days because as joint owners of the horses, there were always things I needed to discuss with Schufro. It was good for me to have someone who could give advice, who also criticised me or pointed out that I was doing too much, riding too much, that such ambitious programmes could be bad for the horses.

"When I saw Gaby for the first time, she was about fifteen, I think. We larked about in the swimming pool and I said to a friend who was with us that she ought to be put to grass for a year or two – then she might grow into a useful filly. She didn't think it was at all funny at the time, but the rest of us laughed. That's all there is to say about it. Later, when she grew up, I took her more seriously. It's good being together."

If ambition is the driving force of success in sport, achieved amibition ought to be the point at which the career comes to an end. Is fulfilment necessarily a thing of a moment? If it isn't, it is hardly possible to explain how it is that for decades a man has sacrificed more than half his free time to a relatively useless pastime – even if, in his case, it has been possible also to combine it with certain commercial, and hence profitable, enterprises. This apart, sport produces nothing tangible. It is basically useless, apart from giving pleasure. It doesn't increase the Gross National Product. And even if it is sometimes maintained these days that successful sport increases a country's reputation, it is a theory difficult to prove and easily demolished.

In Alwin Schockemöhle's case, physical pain comes into it too. Are sportsmen masochists? At the Munich Olympics, the eldest competitor was a seventy-year-old dressage rider from Great Britain. She said she enjoyed riding every day. Of course there are age limits for the performance of certain sports and also biological limits. For riding, the timespan during which one can compete in first class sport is greater than in any other. Anyone who has ever ridden a horse knows that it isn't like relaxing on a live, steerable sofa; there's work to do, laborious strenuous work that makes you sweat. But the physical effort required can hardly be as great as it is in most kinds of sport if men and women are able to compete for universally acknowledged medals and championships at an age when others are usually grandparents, spending their peaceful days in a rocking chair. One would look in vain in the championship tables for a seventy-year-old fencer, a sixty-year-old boxer, a fifty-year-old sprinter or a forty-year-old swimmer. Equally one would look there in vain for an eighteen-year-old rider.

What is the motivation of someone who has already slept in hotel beds throughout the world, who has ridden in all the jumping arenas of the world, who has won all the prizes there are to be won? Is it, in the last analysis, mere habit – being used to the same self-imposed stress, something one can't live without? Fear of the sudden appearance of a vacuum in one's life? Why doesn't one simply stop one day?

Alwin Schockemöhle:

"At the beginning of the seventies I had reached a point where I was absolutely fed up and thinking of an overnight retirement. This was quite a long time before I finally won the European Championship. It was partly my physical condition, partly because I wanted more time with my family. On the one hand the constant pain, on the other a slightly guilty conscience. In addition, I was having a lot of trouble with my horses.

"I have already tried to explain about Donald Rex. Perhaps I should describe my special relationship with him in greater detail. And also the special hopes I had of him, particularly in view of the Munich Olympic Games. It was in 1967 that Hans Pracht had offered me this rather unimpressive gelding at Aachen. At first Pracht had intended him for dressage, but when I tried him out that time in Aachen, Donald did everything I asked of him, and with a calmness I had never seen before in a horse, as well as a technique practically unheard of except after many years of careful dressage schooling. Then came Mexico, and Donald didn't disappoint me there. In 1969, the year after, I doubt if there was a better horse in the world. Obviously I had high hopes for Munich. And then the trouble with his back began and his operation followed. It was all over. You can pretend to yourself for a long time that there's such a thing as bad luck, but in the end you don't believe it yourself any longer. I had no doubts about all I had learnt, nor about my own ability. I was simply fed up.

"At that time, I often toyed with the idea of finishing with top class riding for good. I didn't want to be the eternal runner up. I didn't want to be always waiting for my rivals to make a mistake so that I could beat them. It may sound odd, but there are two ways of winning. One is when you are really in top form and you know for a fact that you are the best. The other is simply when your opponents are not in the same class, when they're out of luck. The results tables make no distinction which was which. You can make yourself believe what you want for quite a while, but deep down, you know it's only yourself you're kidding.

"I didn't want it to go on like that. But then several fortunate circumstances occurred in quick succession, and they persuaded me to go on. The most important of them was a definite improvement in my health. My back was still painful, but I could move normally again. And I could ride too. Wearing a corset feels funny at first, but you get used to it. And once again I had the kind of horses that suit me best and with which I could achieve something. These were Warwick Rex and Santa Monica. Now my successes started giving me a lot of satisfaction again, and if there is any single motivation which makes me want to go on riding, then it's success.

"Of course people ask you about it more and more often as you grow older. Give it up? I know I've been at the game long enough, actually for twenty years. If there is such a thing in sport, then I could say I've done my bit. But who is to say what is one's 'bit'? Does it exist? Hardly, if at all.

In May 1977, however, Schockemöhle announced his retirement from show-jumping. In this interview conducted some time before his announcement he remarked that he would continue while he had good horses, felt fit and enjoyed himself; but when he realised that he couldn't "beat the boys anymore"—Hartwig Steenken, Harvey Smith or David Broome—then he'd like to retire. There could be other reasons such as not having horses of the required standard, or having a recurrence of his back trouble. If all these coincided he would retire before his rivals and colleagues began to notice that his powers were failing. He continued:

"That would be the worst thing as far as I'm concerned, that people should talk about me behind my back and perhaps make fun of me, and I jogging along behind them like a blind old fool; such cases have been known in the past. I don't want people to be sorry for me. Sympathy is horrible if you're the sportsman on the receiving end. Even today I admire Fritz Thiedemann who decided one day to give it all up. He knew he was unlikely ever to repeat his most outstanding performances, so he declared exactly when he would end his long career with all the consequences this entailed. That's what I'd like to do one of these days. It must be terrible if people start telling

80

you it's time to stop, or even ordering you to do so. One sees it so often in other sports, the tennis players who can't win their games, boxers too, and runners who refuse to believe they're finished. It must be particularly galling for footballers, if they've been demi-gods for a good ten years, and then can't even find a club to give them a contract. Away with them – to the scrapyard! No – I'd like to decide for myself.

"Retire. Of course that doesn't mean I'll never ride again, but I wouldn't compete in the big events any more. But I'm certain I'd never give up riding overnight. I'm too much of a 'horsy' type, as they say, to do that. Of course I'll ride at home and cross country, and maybe try out a jump or two occasionally, perhaps school a few horses once in a way. I'd like to have two or three young riders living with us, young people who want to learn and who fit in with my way of life. I'd gladly show them the tricks of the trade. I'd send them to the various trials and be delighted if they started winning.

"I couldn't imagine a life without horses, with the boxes in the stables suddenly empty. An empty stable – I get upset at the very idea. As long as I can afford it, that will never happen."

Methods

The idea of passing on one's experience sounds so simple. There are of course born teachers, coaches who have never won any major championships themselves but who have nevertheless managed to show their pupils how to succeed. There are also champions who have done the same. However, the examples of winners who have not had the gift of handing down their skills are much more numerous. One may call it the discrepancy between theory and practice. Although written descriptions and pictorial representations of riding go far back into history, the "invention" of show jumping is lost in the mists of the past. Did some primitive horseman really assemble an assortment of the obstacles encountered when hunting or riding cross country and actually drag them into the meadow behind his house? Did he do it for no better reason than to show a circle of observers what he and his horses could do? Or did he – and this doesn't sound too farfetched – demonstrate the jumping potential of his horses to prospective buyers, with a view to trying to clinch a sale? If so, the arenas of today which are used for the big events may be nothing more than exhibition grounds, a kind of shop window.

This brings us to the story of the Italian Federico Caprilli, who lived in the second half of the last century and who is "accused" of having formulated riding instructions which could be turned to use for show jumping. Caprilli was a soldier, a cavalry man of course, and the principles he taught were intended as precepts for the cavalry in battle, with the object of winning, that goes without saying. His instructions hardly amount to what may be called a proper system. What has come down to us can easily be understood by the layman. Caprilli hadn't much time for strict dressage, for the beauty of horses on parade. In battle, horses and riders in the front line used to present an imposing picture – but when man had invented gunpowder, the cavalryman also became a splendid target. Caprilli tried to change this from a strategic point of view, so that horse and rider were no longer a sitting target. What he demanded was that riders must adapt themselves to their mounts. Before, it had been the other way about. The rider now had to readjust the balance, keeping in closer relationship with the forward impetus of the horse, and most of all when jumping an obstacle.

In the context of riding history these military-strategic reflections by Federico Caprilli may be taken as the origin and also the explanation of what is known in the jargon of the sport as the "forward Italian seat".

Let us clear up one point, by the way: this graceful way of riding was not wholly approved of in Germany, where the tendency is more towards ordered thoroughness. Germans themselves say that they're a bit heavy-handed when it comes to gracefulness. In this case, however, something happened which must always be considered as a very convincing argument, no matter what differences of opinion there are. The Italians were highly successful. Victories are not always proof that the means used are the right ones, but they do carry conviction. At this point, arguments about theory and practice are always likely to flare up; it's only natural.

The Germans then adopted the idea of the "forward" seat in principle, but added some ideas of their own. A good deal of dressage was incorporated into the "forward seat" technique and everyone admits that herein lies the real secret of equestrianism. The Hanover Cavalry School, with their riders and horses beautifully matched, used to embody to perfection this particular style. And they were almost unbeatable. The proof of it can be read in the Olympic results tables whenever the Germans were allowed to take part. The high spot was undoubtedly at the 1936 Berlin Olympic Games, when this team virtually swept the board in all the equestrian events.

It is readily acknowledged that the success of this method continued virtually without a break when, at the 1952 Olympics in Helsinki, German riders again participated for the first time since 1936. This is explained by the fact that the postwar riders too received their basic training in Hanover, and this was surely the decisive factor. Thiedemann must be quoted as an example. In 1952, he won two bronze medals, one for jumping and one for dressage, an achievement which tends to be forgotten today, and is indeed scarcely credible. He was in many ways a perfectionist. He was also a hard rider, as he himself was ready to admit. In preparing his horses he used means which were forbidden in later years, but he had a plausible explanation for it. In the hands of experts, such aids are no more than support for careful schooling. If a beginner tried to use the same aids, however, they could be cruel. No doubt Thiedemann would also have admitted that the rules drawn up must apply equally to everyone, and may not be "bent" for the sake of any special category.

Basing his schooling on perfect dressage, Thiedemann probably did more in the postwar years for the refinement of the so-called German style of jumping than many of his successors realise or would even admit today. The rule of thumb which lays down the precise point where the horse takes off, to the last centimetre almost, and how it is possible to guide the horse exactly to this spot and at a reasonable speed – these were things he mastered better than practically anyone else at the time. Certainly without this dressage tuition, it would have been impossible to find the point by means of shorter or longer strides. This technique has not always been looked on favourably, since it has been possible to obtain good results with it, even using inferior horses. The criticism has been directed especially at the picture presented in those fractions of a second between holding in the horse and allowing it to shoot forward – what Fritz Thiedemann himself called "the art of brake-and-accelerator play", in which he was a complete master. And here again: the method's success must be considered as a very good argument for it.

There is no doubt that Hans Günter Winkler has refined this technique and indeed he has been credited with inventing it. His thesis that "No one can win the Nations' Cup with time faults" has led to a whole string of Olympic medals.

Although at first glance there are often no apparent similarities between Winkler's cool controlled style, and

Thiedemann's much more powerful, often seemingly brutal reining in of the horse, both are based on the same calculations and the same tactics. Today there are few show jumpers of world class who have not adopted them, and of course there are imitators who try to do something similar without the same expertise or the same grounding. Among those who have long since mastered the art is Alwin Schockemöhle, although he doesn't always achieve his results by exactly the same means.

Alwin Schockemöhle:

"Everyone has his own methods for achieving success, and I have mine. And of course I can only pass on my personal methods to others – it can't be something other riders do, which I've only watched or read about. It's an odd feeling when you're asked for advice for the first time. It's a kind of shock and it's only later that you think: well I never! There you were, thinking you were still a learner yourself, and suddenly up comes someone and wants you to teach him! You feel rather flattered at the time but it makes you thoughtful too.

"I enjoy teaching young people. You get a certain satisfaction when they start making their mark, even when they beat you! You feel it's your victory too in a small way. It also makes me believe that the method I've shown them can't be so bad after all. Gert Wiltfang, for instance, had great talent from the start, a fellow with tremendous power and the best eye a show jumper can possibly have. He also has the necessary drive, he wants to learn. Even without me he would probably have become a good show jumper, but perhaps I was able to help him to get there a little sooner. Maybe he got to the top a bit too quickly. It was no favour to him when he found himself tipped as the winner for the individual event in Munich in 1972. It was extremely difficult for him. And I'm sure it was even harder for him to get over the shock. It has taken him a long time to do so, and it led to a lot of trouble afterwards. I'm glad for him these days when I see that he's got over it and is doing well again.

"Another of my pupils is Dutch, Johan Hein. Already I consider him one of the best riders in the world, although he's still comparatively young. He only needs the horses on which he can win. It's always the same story. The best rider is no use without the right horse. On the other hand, the best possible horse may be there, but no one can ride him properly. All the same, I'm always delighted when I see people progressing, when my kind of training and my riding methods bring results. I certainly don't want to sing my own praises, but if in years to come someone should say: 'That man rides like Schockemöhle used to', I'll feel quite proud of it. And anyone who doesn't understand this has no idea what sport is about, nor indeed what life is about.

"Every human being needs recognition for his work – and so do horses. As you grow older, you can quickly differentiate between recognition and flattery. Recognition has nothing to do with friendship, which has already been discussed. There are people whom everyone must acknowledge as being good at their job. I would also include here people with whom I have little in common personally, or who have lost touch with me in the course of time. But you must be able to distinguish between the good and the bad, in the sense of pretentiousness. If you can do this, you will always be accepted as a teacher or a coach. Yet very often it is not easy to make a distinction. One needs a lot of experience for this. With any method one must assume that only results in competitions prove its value."

A lot of bad things have been said about the draw-rein method used by Alwin Schockemöhle. His style was far from classic and caused a lot of hostile comment.

Alwin Schockemöhle:

"I have imitated something from every rider I admire. That doesn't mean that my style is a hotchpotch – my own individuality and personality guarantee that! But I have learned a lot from a lot of people. The combination of all these examples woven into my own potential obviously has brought results. It is difficult to explain my system. The problem is that most people only see that my horses go deep, that is: to the outside. They then say: 'He managed this by using his draw-rein'. Yet that is not so! I work mainly with my legs and as little as possible with my hands. Pulling is no use. It merely spoils the horse. I have no weight in my hands. The horses do not fear my hands; their own impulse drives them ahead of me. The draw-rein is poison, but most riders use it constantly; if I ride a horse for an hour I use the draw-

86

rein at the most for three minutes. People have also told me: 'You are too strong and your method of riding is so hard, so that only big heavy horses survive with you.' I don't think I have to defend myself. The people who really know my way of riding know that it is not a feat of strength."

It becomes evident from the above that the total training of horses is judged by the principles of dressage. The methods are the same, but the results differ. Alwin talks about working from the backhand, the loosening of the back, the encouragement to the horse to obey, just like any other top dressage rider does. Dressage takes more than ninety per cent of the training time. There is no jumping at home with experienced horses, only dressage and gymnastics.

Such a way of doing things requires very good previous basic training. Schooling in Warendorf with the West German top dressage team and participation in military training have given Alwin the basis he needs to become what he is now. He admits at once that this basis is not the only important thing.

"There has to be talent. An eye for obstacles is innate. I only know one rider who did not have an eye for obstacles, but who has acquired this by endless training – my own brother Paul. This as a rule is impossible. There has to be talent and this talent has to be developed by endless practice."

Disappointments

Disappointments must always be reckoned with in sport. Disappointments are usually due to inflated expectations of one's ability. Disappointments are certainly found more often among sportsmen of roughly equal quality, of whom only one can win, than among those who are glad just to be allowed to take part. Thiedemann once said he found it more galling to be placed second than eighth.

Alwin Schockemöhle:

"Of course I have had my disappointments. But there is a distinction to be made here between those that are due to human failure and those that are caused by the horse's failure. When I look back on my sporting career, my only real disappointment was at the Tokyo Olympics in 1964. At that time, in spite of having only one horse, Freiherr, I thought I had a good chance. On that occasion, Germany found they hadn't a complete team in Japan. Hans Winkler was to ride Cornelia and Hermann Schridde had Ilona. I had prepared myself and Freiherr as never before – or since, probably. Perhaps we trained too strenuously. From this distance in time, it's hard to say. However that may be, when suddenly Freiherr was injured, there was I without a horse.

"Schridde and I had taken only one reserve horse between us, the gelding Dozent. He had once belonged to me, but Schridde took him over. At first sight, this prearranged agreement appeared to be a reasonable one. It's a long way to Tokyo, and one reserve horse between two riders seemed enough to make such a journey. Who would have dreamed that two of our best horses would have to drop out? Hermann, of course, had the first choice. After all, Dozent was his horse. Felizitas had been taken along as a spare for Winkler's Cornelia, and that was how Kurt Jarasinski, who was actually only the

When Alwin Schockemöhle took over the family estate, he was just twenty years old.
"I invested every penny of my savings in it – I worked like mad"

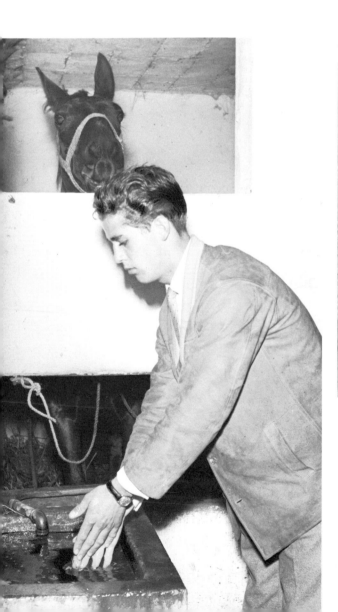

"It was then I decided I'd make a million by the time I was 30, and I'd stop working at 40. I shan't stick to at least one of these aims. Everyone must have a purpose in life"

Gaby and Alwin Schockemöhle in 1967, at the opening of the Jumping Derby, Hamburg, looking forward to the birth of their first child, Alexandra
Alwin Schockemöhle has three production plants for steel reinforcement mesh. "I visit the customers, and my brother-in-law 'Louis' Willenborg sees to the commercial side of the business"

*Schockemöhle is not without a touch of
pride in his achievements: his beautiful
house, Alexandra, Frank and Christoph,
his success, and also the respect he has won*

"My home is my castle"

reserve, got the gold medal. And Schridde on Dozent won the silver in the individual event.

"I sat in the stands, watching. I must admit now that it was a rotten feeling. I was glad that they had won, but I was also disappointed that I wasn't there in the arena with them. One can talk of bad luck. What's the use? I must say now that all the three horses we had entered had actually passed their peak and were no longer up to the very great strain. Naturally, it was also to some extent my own fault. If only I had worked Freiherr a little less hard, if only I had taken greater care, if, if, if . . .

"It's all over and done with now.

"That's how it is with the big championships. They occur only every few years. You have to be prepared exactly to the day, to the hour even. If you've done everything possible and then out of the blue, something unforeseen occurs which makes nonsense of many years of hard work, then you are entitled to feel disappointed. As I said, as an example of disappointment, I can only think of what happened in Tokyo.

"Everything else which could be so described goes back to my very early days in riding. When you have some wins to your credit, you believe it must go on like that for ever more. Every mistake is considered as Fate playing a dirty trick, and you don't notice that the fault was yours. You consider yourself a superman and all doors must open before you, and you're surprised when it doesn't happen like that. This is probably the most difficult part when you're serving your apprenticeship. Of course there are disappointments, but if you can't get over them, you'll never reach the top. At this stage, disappointments are very beneficial. You have to come down to earth and this is an excellent starting position. You can't climb mountains from the top.

"From such experiences you develop a routine, which is no more than a cool appraisal of the facts of a situation and relating them to your own actual potential. It incurs a certain degree of risk, which must always be accepted, even when you have already established a routine and acquired experience. This applies especially to show jumping. Things are different with, say, a hundred metre sprinter. If he has an off day, he finishes third. So what? Tomorrow he tries again and wins. After the victory, no one mentions his previous defeat. But if I make a silly mistake at a show, I'm suddenly out of the running. I remember Hartwig Steenken at the Munich Olympic Games. He came to grief because of a stupid error which he'd never have made in the ordinary way. Had it not been for this, he would have won the gold medal easily, without even a jump off. He knows this himself.

"In my opinion, this is why riding is very useful as general education. One can learn how to lose more easily than elsewhere, and there's no sense in venting your disappointment on the horse. Every rider knows the moment he's made a mistake – if not in the arena, then at home during training. You learn how to control yourself, or rather, it becomes a habit. If you have to live with frequent peaks and troughs, you don't get hurt so badly. And you don't take things to heart so much. In show jumping, it can happen that you've really done all the right things and then suddenly it starts pouring and the horse slips a trifle, he barely brushes against the pole and the wretched thing falls to the ground. The other competitors completed their rounds before the rain – they knicked the pole hard with a resounding thwack, and it slipped back into place. Should you rail against Fate, and curse your luck?

"When you've been at the game as long as I have, you play it more coolly, you face facts with greater equanimity, you don't get so excited. There are a whole range of words one uses – 'Fate', 'form on the day', 'luck' – I don't think much of any of them. That's how it is, and that's all there is to it. The next day perhaps I'll be the one who's more successful. There are things you can't calculate. There must always be a certain percentage of risk as I said before. It would be a bad thing if you could predict results in sport to such an extent that they could be worked out on a computer. The fascination of the unknown is a big part of sport."

If luck plays a part in sport, then one must say that Schockemöhle hasn't always been on good terms with Fortune. Incidentally, this is a compliment, although not an obvious one. No eminent person, no matter what his field, can boast or would like to boast that he owes his position to luck. It may sometimes contribute in part to success, but it cannot be a reliable partner. Any person who has been counted among the world's best for decades, can hardly have built his career on the sandy foundations of luck.

Alwin Schockemöhle has never indulged in day-dreams. He tends rather to calculate dispassionately, drawing conclusions for the next occasion, weighing up the odds and puzzling things out.

Alwin Schockemöhle:

"I'm not a gambler in the ordinary sense of the word. I'd never lose my head gambling as many people do. I always think things out. Of course I have gambled at times, and the story they tell of me is, in a way, true.

"It's absolutely logical. I put 10 D-marks on red, and black comes up. Next time I put 20 D-marks on red, and black comes up again. Then I put 40 D-marks on red. Red must come up again some time. All I have to do is keep doubling the stake every time. After a while, this can amount to a tidy sum, but I mustn't weaken. If I gamble at all, it's only on simple straightforward chances, black or red, odds or evens. And when I've lost, I double the sum until I win. It's certainly not inspired playing, nor is it intelligent advice on how to get rich at roulette. But as I've already said, I'm no gambler. I always like to keep the risk in perspective. I prefer to plan and have things under my control. This applies to my whole life – including my business life."

Work

A man whose outstanding career as a sportsman is due to his realistic thinking can't suddenly behave differently in other aspects of his life. The European Championship which he won in 1975 is a very good example of his practical approach. On this occasion he had at his disposal the grey gelding Rex the Robber, a magnificent jumper, powerful but sensitive, highly responsive to external influences, but for this reason also unreliable. Instead, Alwin Schockemöhle saddled the much less brilliant Warwick, a nicely behaved chestnut, unpretentious although thoroughly well schooled, that goes without saying. Therein lies the secret of success – forgoing the external glitter in favour of safety first. If there are any lessons to be learnt for life from sport then surely one can learn lessons from life, which may be applied to sport. The successful businessman Alwin Schockemöhle has put it into practice in this instance by applying his business experience to his riding. You don't get anywhere if you rely on luck and glamour.

Sometime or other – he must have been in his middle twenties, and the time was late at night – he once said among friends that by the time he was thirty, he would like to be worth one million D-marks. And that when he reached forty, he would give up work altogether.

Alwin Schockemöhle:

"I've already made the point in connection with gambling – I don't take great risks in business either. I try to do business where I believe there are markets. There are always opportunities for making a fortune – but then, they also carry the risk of losing even more. I don't think much of that. I prefer to steer a middle course. Because of this, I've certainly made less profit than my competitors, but I sleep more soundly for it. I see myself as an ordinary respectable citizen.

"Business is sometimes very much like sport. In both cases success is an effective motivation. You think time and again what would happen if you retired – let someone else carry on what you have started. After all, once I'm dead, I can't take it with me. But then you think that having invested your money somewhere or other, you want to watch it make a profit. And with the profit you've made, you'd like to make further investments – it's a vicious circle. All the time there's more work to be done, more responsibility, more commitments, it keeps getting harder to stop. Does anyone like giving up a business he's built up from scratch?

"Sometimes I remember what I thought and said when I was twenty, what I was planning at the time and how much of it I've accomplished. But this is a phase every young man goes through. At twenty, you think a man of forty is an aged grandfather – and the day comes when you're touching forty yourself, and you realise you don't feel anything like a grandfather yet. And when you notice that youngsters do in fact look on you as an old man, it only makes you laugh. Perhaps that's what's called experience. You can learn almost anything in life, but you can't learn how it actually feels to be older, but not yet old. You can only discover that from personal experience. I couldn't imagine a life without work; it's an essential part of me, and it's also one of the things I enjoy doing. Sometimes it means great fatigue. But then all I do is sleep it off in a couple of days, and afterwards I lie awake in the small hours and think of something new, of improvements to be made, or how to obtain greater productivity.

"I must have been lucky to start with. All I knew was how to run a farm. My brother-in-law Louis Willenburg, who is now my business partner, helped me very much at the time. I had already realised that sport isn't everything, that one can't spend one's whole life on it. I'd often wondered what I would do when it was all over one day; what would I do then for a living? I also considered how I could make use later on of all the connections I had established through sport. And I admit frankly that the name I had made for myself as a rider opened many doors which I'm sure would have otherwise remained shut.

101

"Louis and I started many things together and so far we've been reasonably successful. At first my reputation was more useful than it is today, now that I'm well established in this particular line of business. That's always the case when someone wants to start up and break new ground. Today we produce steel reinforcement mesh for building purposes. We have four factories in production. Of course we didn't invent it – it was already on the market when we started, and people were selling it. We came to the business green and inexperienced – but we offered good quality and probably keen prices. In any event, we were successful.

"For a time I also had a chicken farm, as well as a peat processing firm in the Bremen region. When we started in steel, we scraped together all our capital – I had the advice of my brother-in-law who seems to have a good business flair – and as I mentioned, my contribution was a fairly well-known name. That was all. Nor did I ask for help from my family to make a start, not even from my father-in-law as many people believed. He has nothing to do with my business interests, although I dare say he would have given me credit if I'd asked him.

"In my view it's wrong to mix business with family matters. It's an additional source of satisfaction to me that I'm not dependent on anyone, nor am I under any obligations. The business was our doing alone and our co-operation is first class. While my brother-in-law supervised the production side, I went the rounds. I got to know many people, talked things over with them, learning all the time and trying to make improvements. That's all.

"One last word on the subject of the business world: you must never do things by halves. Otherwise it's better not to start. There's no sense in sitting around, waiting for things to fall into your lap. The people who later became partners or customers wouldn't have bought anything from me if I'd given them a lecture on how to train horses for show jumping, or what it feels like to stand in front of the crowd with the national anthem being played. I had to learn the business like any other beginner. And I had to learn more about the goods I had to sell than the buyers knew. That's not as easy as it sounds, but you must persevere. As I said, you can't do things by halves."

Without Illusions

Over the last few decades, competitive riding and especially show jumping has undoubtedly tended to move in the direction of circus performances. Nevertheless, there remains a big gap between the two. This can be demonstrated by the enormously increased number of leisure riders, a fact which no one could have predicted not so long ago. The theory that leisure riding is really only the result of successful horse shows is too flimsy to be taken seriously. A cross country runner is motivated as little by the 10,000 m. Olympic finals as a week-end skier is by watching a world champion on the television screen, weaving in and out of a forest of obstacles as he hurtles down the snow-covered slope.

The great interest that spectators continue to show in any kind of equestrian sport can only be considered to a small degree as evidence of affection for horses and what they can do. Often it is much more on a par with a bull-fight, a boxing match or a big football game. It is the appetite for an exciting spectacle, and not the desire to observe something that might be of personal benefit at some future date. In short, not to learn but to experience.

The major events in show jumping – the Olympic Games, the World and European Championships, as well as a number of international meetings, the so-called Official Meetings (C.S.I.O.) – may be considered objectively as exhibition grounds for horse breeders who, through a lengthy process of selection, have created a species of horse particularly suited to this sport.

The large number of first class riders, and the even greater number of first class horses, have presented the world's course architects with more and more problems. Do I build a course for fast horses, or only for high jumpers? Do I create what the experts call "fair" jumps, or design what might be considered traps, in order to sift the wheat from the chaff? It is highly unlikely that anyone ever again will construct a course like the one built in Mexico City in 1968. Quite apart from the time limits which, it has since been confirmed, were grossly miscalculated, it included a series of hidden traps.

Nowadays it would appear that only in exceptional cases would show jumpers with their many commitments force their horses frantically from show to show as was the case not so long ago. This may be due to the fact that horses have become more valuable in recent years. When reasonably good jumpers could be bought for 30,000 or 40,000 D-marks, people weren't quite so careful with them. Provided the horse remained fit, the purchase price could be paid off in two or three years. Today's prices are several times higher. One is more cautious with 150,000 D-marks. A cold, an inflammation of the sinews, and bang goes your money. This need not be caused by overexertion. Fritz Ligges, the best rider in the German gold medal team in Munich in 1972 was walking his mighty grey Robin on the lunge when the horse hurt himself so badly that death came as a welcome relief from lingering pain. If Ligges had sold the gelding after his successful performance, there would have been cries of protest throughout the land. Afterwards everyone was sorry for this fine rider. He hadn't enough money left to pay the vet's bills.

Whether the big competitions are in fact nothing but a market place for horsedealers is something of a sore point. *Alwin Schockemöhle:*
"It's all a matter of cool business calculation and I'll try to explain it in purely commercial terms.

"Every sportsman nowadays who wants to be at the top of a major sport needs backing from somewhere, which we show jumpers simply do not have. Without money, no horse and no rider can survive. I can't buy oats, I can't even buy horses. So I must see what can be done.

"There is one basic misunderstanding which must be cleared up for a start. In print, it says for instance that the Aachen Grand Prix is worth 40,000 D-marks. Put like this, it's totally misleading for the man in the street. People are made to believe that the winner actually pockets 40,000 D-marks, and that's a nice day's takings by most standards. In fact, it works out that the winner may receive 5,000 D-marks and the remainder is shared between the runners up. From my personal experience I can state categorically that I couldn't finance any kind of stable at all from competition winnings; no matter how you juggle with the figures, it just isn't possible.

"The actual balance sheet looks quite different. Assuming that I pay out something like 100,000 D-marks for a good horse, that in itself, for what one might call one's essential equipment, is a sum far beyond what is required in other sports. If he turns out to be a good horse, it is possible to collect maybe between 20,000 and 30,000 D-marks in a good year. If all goes well and my health remains good, if I have the time to attend the various meetings, if the horse doesn't fall ill and if he retains his form, I just about get my initial outlay back after four or five years. Then it's said I'm doing well out of it – but in what way, I'd like to know? I could safely invest the same money at ten per cent, which would yield 10,000 D-marks per annum. So using 100,000 D-marks as working capital for four or five years would have increased the original amount considerably.

"Where then is the huge profit I'm supposed to be making from show jumping? Furthermore, it is only realistic to assume that the normal life expectancy of the average horse in this sport is perhaps four to five years. If I only get my money back, I have in effect made a loss. And this, mind you, is in an ideal case. I have assumed that the horse remains in good health and so do I, and that we're both successful.

"From a purely commercial point of view, and working on a figure of ten per cent interest, i.e. 10,000 D-marks, plus 25,000 depreciation and also 12,000 to 15,000 maintenance costs, I am left with 50,000 D-marks. So a horse costing 100,000 D-marks originally, would have to collect 50,000 D-marks per annum in prize money. Now get down the yearbooks and see which horse has done this. Looked at this way, the illusions vanish. On a purely commercial calculation, only a lunatic would invest his money like that. From the business point of view, it's a loss maker!

"Of course we try to keep the risk low, and everyone

knows how. We go out of our way to buy younger horses which don't involve so much expense. With hard work every day and an infinite amount of patience, it may perhaps be possible to bring these young horses to the pitch where they improve their performance. If later they make the grade, and provided someone is interested, you may be able – possibly – to resell them.

"If you look up the tables in the year books, it's easy to see that there are scarcely twenty horses who have won 20,000 D-marks. In West Germany alone 20,000 to 30,000 horses are presented for the various trials. So it's easy to work out that all the rest are working at a financial loss. I'm perfectly sure that there isn't another sport in the world where the sportsman's financial resources are under such strain.

"Perhaps three of my horses earn their keep, and this doesn't mean only their feed, but also the necessary staff. Without staff, I can't attend to my own business. But if I only ride and deal in horses, then I can no longer be considered as an amateur. It's a vicious circle! In addition to these three horses, I have at least another twenty in the stables, which I'm forced to maintain and school, and try to make good horses out of them. They eat just as much as the others and they need just as much care and attention so that means more staff, more fodder and so on.

"I've never had a penny of subsidy, even when I hold the horses back so that on the occasion they can be entered 'for Germany' – no contribution to their feed, nothing. On the contrary, there are always fresh expenses, entry fees, registration fees and stabling.

"Not so long ago, my brother Paul was at the Münster meeting where he entered several horses, including some very young ones. At the end of the meeting he had paid 1,800 D-marks in entry and registration fees and he had won 45 D-marks! This is something one must try to bring home to people. I readily admit that in this instance Paul didn't do very well – but what about the many other riders to whom this is always happening? You must include them too if you want to arrive at any valid conclusion. In no sport do the rules lay down different standards for the successful and the less successful. And the latter are the majority in any sport.

"Think of the sheer effort required simply to find a

horse that looks promising. I know riders who arrive at a meeting at five o'clock on a Sunday morning, and at eight o'clock on Monday morning they're on their way again, because they've just heard about a fantastic horse somewhere else, and they can't wait to try him out. No one mentions this, because relatively few people know of it, and the rest simply haven't given it any thought. Does anyone ever find a horse ready trained? These are the points which make show jumping basically different from other sports. I'm not complaining about it. All I ask for is understanding."

Who's it for?

Who the devil does Alwin Schockemöhle ride for? For whom does he make himself suffer so? (And in this case, quite apart from the time spent and the strenuous training, the suffering is literal as well as metaphorical.) For himself? For his association? For his team? For West Germany?

Alwin Schockemöhle:

"I can't say. For no one. For everyone. Both statements are right and both are wrong. There are situations from which I derive both satisfaction and pleasure, in a purely personal sense, I admit. Personal success is something I want. Perhaps we've been chatting in the stables or the collecting ring, there's been a bit of teasing, leg-pulling, then someone makes what sounds like a joke about you, but it's really meant seriously and you immediately say to yourself: I'll show him! Something like that can act as a positive spur. There are trainers in other fields of sport who do this deliberately in order to goad their pupils to success. It's probably sound psychology. You don't realise it at the time usually. It's only later on reflection that you become aware of it.

"But of course there are other situations where you are forced to think of the team. And for us riders, the team is always synonymous with Germany and the Nations' Cup. Here the decision isn't always so simple. For instance, on the day before the Nations' Cup in Aachen, say, an important event is due to take place which you would like to win. You've inspected the course and believe you've a good chance; the prize money for the runners up is also good enough, so that you could reckon fairly safely on getting through the whole meeting without financial loss. And then other considerations arise. If I ride my best horse in the individual trial, perhaps it

108

will be too tired next day for the Nations' Cup and make a mistake. So you must decide if you'll seize your only chance of having a clear round, or save the horse for the following day, when what is at stake is the honour of your country, but there's no money in it for you personally. Which shall it be?

"I believe that all good riders in this country have a sound approach when they're faced with this dilemma. If it were not so, our team would hardly be considered one of the best in the world, if not the best. Somehow or other everyone is proud to be allowed to ride as a member of the team. One ought to look at it in the same light as, for instance, Franz Beckenbauer, the footballer, does, when he's asked to play for Germany. To say it's an honour may sound a bit highflown, but that's what it is.

"Of course there have been differences of opinion on such occasions, but if a person prefers not to forgo his personal chances, he must drop out of the team event. On the other hand there are horses that can perform well two days running. In case of doubt you must trust the rider who knows the horse and can make a better judgment.

"Basically, everyone is prepared to push his own interests into the background to some extent. If there were any doubt, I personally would rest the horse, so as to spare him for the following day.

'To return to the original point – if you're asked whether you ride for yourself or for your country, you can't answer with a simple yes or no. I believe in a compromise. Of course everyone wants to cut a good figure on such occasions, but why? It's good for the team, but not for the individual. That time in Mexico, the day of the Nations' Cup, when Hermann Schridde's horse Dozent had a bad time and knocked over everything in sight – on that occasion I was the best individual rider, and four years before, under the rules then prevailing, I would have won the gold medal. However, we definitely thought only of the team in that instance, and how we could make good Dozent's mistakes.

"No. Anyone who has decided to go in for top class sport has at the same time assumed an obligation also to perform for his country. Whoever works his way to the top in any competitive sport does it to some extent for

patriotic reasons. I think that goes for all the sportsmen
I know."

The Value of Success

It is obvious that no one can do without praise in-definitely. To be a star, one needs the support of the mass media, and it is probably true that the media tend to attach importance to occasions which do not necessarily warrant it. Conversely, it can be said that they do not mention events that deserve to be reported.

Alwin Schockemöhle:

"There are events which a sportsman views differently from a reporter – sometimes differently from the judges. I have been praised for wins which I knew in my heart of hearts were not worth mentioning. This may be due simply to the classic name of the trials. No account is taken of who the other competitors were, and the fact that my horse was by far the best of the starters may be totally ignored. But suddenly you see your name in the list of winners going back for fifty years maybe, and the praise lavished is out of all proportion. All the same, I'd be lying if I didn't admit it makes you feel good.

"The Olympic Games are an extreme instance of this. The fact that they take place only once in four years has of course a bearing on the fact that a gold medal there is valued more highly than any other distinction. In this respect, Rosi Mittermaier is a very good example. The previous races she had won may well have been more difficult than the Innsbruck ones; after all, she'd been competing for ten years, before this unbroken row of successes. She had seen it all before, one can be sure of that. She herself valued her World Cup more than her Olympic medals. The World Cup, she said, was proof of her superiority for a whole season. From the sportsman's point of view, this is right. But the public will always remember her as 'Golden Rosi from Innsbruck', and only ski fans will add that she also won the World Cup.

Who remembers today the World Cup winners before her? No one. What is the source of Toni Sailer's and Jean-Claude Killy's popularity? It isn't simply that they were world champions and have won so many races, but because they won gold medals at the Olympic Games.

"Fame comes when all these things are happening together. The popular – or popularised – competition, the exciting contest, the winner, the whole population agog as they watch the television screen at home – nothing unites people more than a good cliff-hanger! Here's another example. Until the end of time, Hans Günter Winkler will be associated with his legendary ride on Halla at the Stockholm Olympics. Who speaks of his World Championships these days? And they weren't exactly walkovers either.

"One shouldn't necessarily consider these competitions in sporting terms as the highlights of a career. They are mainly a reward for overcoming much greater difficulties way back in the past.

"There have been nights when I've gone to bed feeling really proud of winning an event. And next day, there may have been no more than a line or two about it in the newspapers. And there were other occasions when I had a walkover, and the whole world got excited about my win. The honest value of a victory is something only the competitor himself can assess; it depends on so many things. If I happen to feel rotten that day and not really fit, and if I win all the same, this victory means much more to me personally than if I had been feeling really well. But I can't go up to all and sundry and tell them. It would only annoy your rivals, for whoever wants to be beaten by a sick man? Nor can you expect reporters, from their point of view as observers, to appreciate the precise difficulties you have to contend with.

"Everything hinges on the dimensions of the obstacles and the distance between the jumps. For many laymen, this is as incomprehensible as the intricacies of the slalom are to me. It was said of one skier that he memorised the precise downhill run in advance – that he had, as it were, already completed the course mentally many times before. In spite of all my experience and a certain detachment I have attained, I always catch myself going round the arena several times in my mind before the big events. It's a fresh adventure every time. This, of course, is due to the fact that every course is constructed differently, because every course builder likes to devise something as new and original as possible. Sometimes the obstacles are closer together or wider apart, the space between varies and so does the time allowed and the order in which the obstacles are placed. And one of the most important things is the choice of horse. Personally I prefer big horses. Then I may need only two strides between the jumps of a double combination, which with a smaller horse, I'd need three. If you enter two different horses in the same competition, you have to memorise two different rounds.

"As I've said, one must be able to differentiate between those triumphs that really deserve the name, and other competitions which anyone could have won. Nevertheless, I must admit that it's the latter which are mentioned repeatedly and which contribute to becoming famous, to becoming a star, or call it what you like. But the others count more among ourselves. At a not very important meeting, perhaps, someone or other comes along and jumps the most difficult round imaginable, and we all take off our hats to him. This in turn opens up a new question. Which praise gives more satisfaction, that of your main rival, or that of the public? I can't say. I like both.

"A comparison with other sports? This is hardly possible. A short distance sprinter knows exactly what he's in for, just those hundred metres. He can train for years at home, he can use the same surface, the same compound material, the same shoes. He knows before he leaves home if he's good enough or not. He can read it off on the stopwatch.

"At the Olympic Games we are allowed to see the arena for the first time at seven o'clock on the morning of the day. Until then we haven't the faintest idea what's in store for us, what will be demanded of us. We don't know anything about the distances between the jumps, if they're right or wrong. I don't even know whether the horse I've prepared will be able to manage it at all. Neither do I know whether the oxers have been built higher or wider, and I can't know if the ground is hard or soft, or how deep it is. We riders know nothing in advance except who designed the arena and who built it. From that you can, at best, imagine roughly how the whole thing looks, but only if you've previously ridden a course constructed by the same person. By merely inspecting the course at seven o'clock in the morning, many a rider realises whether or not he can win. And he also knows in that same moment whether or not all the work of the last few years has been in vain.

"It may sound odd, but in certain respects, I think that show jumping may be compared with a game of football. The uncertainty there is also very great. How often has the favourite team turned up somewhere and been beaten quite unexpectedly? How can it be explained? The experts say it has something to do with their 'form on the day' – they're always bumping into each other, they miss the ball altogether, or don't kick it straight. It depends on so many things, which may have been tried out a thousand times, but are wholly fortuitous in the end. On one occasion, someone kicks a ball from a distance of thirty metres straight into the top left corner of the net, and all the world talks of a masterly shot. But if the same player had placed his foot a millimetre to left or right, the ball would have missed by ten metres and everyone would have sworn at him! No one can plan a football game so that during the tenth minute the ball will bounce at a certain height, either from the left or the right; the player must cope with the situation as it arises and make a lightning decision. He must react and react correctly. And that is what I must do too, at seven o'clock in the morning on the final day of the Olympics, for example, one hour before the Nations' Cup begins. For this reason I appreciate the uncertainties of a game of football more than those encountered by a runner, jumper or swimmer.

"Uncertainty – this is one of the factors that makes sport so attractive. Incidentally, it plays an even bigger rôle in boxing, especially at major tournaments such as the Olympic Games, when one has to fight a different opponent every day. I think I would have enjoyed boxing, or at least I'd have liked to try it. I never had the opportunity, and I dare say I might have given it up, because you do get hurt now and then, but I rather like the idea of it. I'd have liked to discover if my reactions were

114

quicker than someone else's, if I could have got the better of an opponent by a combination of technique and strength.

"What's the use? It's only a pipe dream. I'm probably too old for it now. But I do think about it sometimes."

Tradition—or "Old Hat"?

Alwin Schockemöhle's sporting career has been based on more than just his riding prowess. People were saying a long time ago that he always wanted his own way, something his fellow-riders didn't always take to kindly. He was not too fastidious when it came to what he believed to be superfluous or obsolete. He is no respecter of sacred cows. He has never been two-faced in his friendships. He has never kowtowed to anyone, but in his time he has achieved a great deal.

Besides, he tends to be impatient and he doesn't like using roundabout methods of persuasion. During all the negotiations and discussions arranged at his prompting, he has used the same tactics as those which have distinguished him in the saddle. He tries to go straight to the point. At the same time, he has been so provocative that sometimes sparks flew. In the days when he had nothing to show except his well-developed self-assurance – no major title, nor an aristocratic background which was useful for riders then, not even much money – he went straight to the powers that be and told them what he thought of them. The way he has gained the support of the media can only be admired. He has walked out when he thought it would serve a purpose. Not only has he registered a firm veto to certain unacceptable proposals, but he has replaced them with constructive suggestions. On his initiative, interest groups came into being which were much more than mere cliques. He spurned protection at a time when others were only too glad to take advantage of it.

Many of the changes he carried through appeared at first glance to be designed to further his own selfish ends. Only in the course of years did it emerge that the same way of thinking was also beneficial for his successors. It

116

must be admitted that his ideas haven't always been right. But at least he has set about changing things, and triggered off trains of thought which may have occurred to others before him but which they never actually formulated. He attacked regulations which had been tolerated for many years. It is a remarkable but very common trait in people that they recognise what is wrong, but from fear of those in high places, or from sheer resignation, they do not think of taking them up with the appropriate authority. These are the armchair strategists, so to speak.

There was one outmoded championship rule which Schockemöhle went on attacking until it was changed. The leadership of the association had been traditionally hierarchic until he forced it to greater democracy. One example will suffice. He demanded permission to take part in major events abroad, often connected with big prize money; and this not only for himself, but also for others who felt at a disadvantage.

If he stirred up trouble for himself and for others in his efforts to demolish the old established order, it must be seen vis-à-vis the tradition that still bedevils riding in many respects and can be a burden to it. As a farmer or a businessman, Alwin Schockemöhle would hardly have been accepted in a German riding team before the war, unless he had given up these activities and become an officer. The Olympic results tables of riding events since 1912 are very revealing. They are full of names from the aristocracy, and if one happens to find anyone of less exalted social origin, he was certain to be a high-ranking cavalry officer. The Swedish N.C.O. Petrus Kastenmann has already been mentioned. For a short period in 1956, he was made an officer so that he could take part in the three-day event in Stockholm – and after all, he won! This is only one example, and not even the most telling.

Where as in no other walk of life would anyone dream of addressing a high-ranking officer long retired as "General!", it remains the custom among riders even today. After all, the title is no more than an indication of the pecking order in an honourable profession, i.e. the army. But in equestrian circles, it is considered rather as a qualification, some thing like an academic degree.

Even at the beginning of the seventies, after the pre-

Olympic three-day eventing trials in Munich, an officer of the former cavalry school in Hanover got very excited over the fact that the arena party consisted of young soldiers doing their military service. He reprimanded them for the length of their hair, and said it made him "feel ashamed of ever having worn uniform". In Switzerland, a rider was suspended because for a joke he had shaved the left side of his beard. Incidentally, he was locked up later, and not entirely without justification, since he carried his personal argument with the judges to the point of physical assault. Although the amended Competition Regulations of the German Equestrian Association were approved as late as 1975, the regulation dress is still the traditional red coat for show jumpers, and the top hat for dressage riders.

These items may contribute to the presentation of a charming picture, but in no way do they tally with the idea that clothing should meet the functional requirements of the sport being practised. At the Bavarian championships, again in 1975, when, because of the heatwave, the competitors were allowed to take off their jackets, this fact got more column inches than the actual performance of the winners. And it did nothing to prevent the raising of eyebrows by disapproving visitors, who are devoted to tradition and formality.

It is important to consider these points as a whole to show why it is that young people today are provoked into voicing their protest and indeed are forced to do so. And remarks like: "Why don't they go and play football instead?" stem from such tremendous arrogance, that they are bound to create opposition.

In the sixties, when the number of horses in Germany was rapidly diminishing, together with the popularity of equestrian sports, there might have been the opportunity to re-think all these questions. However, the recent "discovery" of riding as a widely practised leisure pursuit has now made this superfluous. The number of horses is increasing again and so is the number of riders. A democratisation plain for all to see is inevitable.

118

The Organisation
under Fire

These considerations must have influenced Alwin Schockemöhle, then in his early twenties, to try to reform some of the dust-covered traditions which he considered were old-fashioned and wholly out of date. Later, of course, after he had achieved a measure of success, it was easier for him to voice his opinions, when he could afford to call meetings, when he knew what his rights were and, if necessary, how to invoke the law.

An earlier acquaintanceship may also have played a part here. At the time when Schockemöhle was a dressage-rider, intending to take part in three-day eventing, he shared a room at Warendorf with Reiner Klimke, a Westphalian, who became one of the world's best dressage riders. Later, Klimke took a degree in law, and by temperament (Westphalians have a reputation for obstinacy) as well as by profession, he was very well equipped to conduct legal arguments. He and Schockemöhle probably learned a great deal from one another, even if they sometimes went their separate ways afterwards. They were both disappointed when others were selected for the three-day event at the 1956 Olympics; they would have liked to ride together on that occasion. It could well have been then that the secret idea of changing things was born. Although at that time their ideas may have sprung from somewhat selfish interests, they developed into trains of thought which were also of use to others.

Alwin Schockemöhle:
"I appear before the public. This gives the public the right to criticise me. I also ride for my association, and so the association too has the right to criticise me. And I in turn reserve the right to criticise my critics. Everyone who appears in public is entitled to this kind of in-

119

dependence, no matter who he is, actor, politician or sportsman.

"I've always tried to stand up for the rights of riders. This may sound highminded and altruistic, but it's really true. How often has it happened that we were sitting together somewhere, complaining about this and that, and then, when one of the officials has joined us round the table, the complaints disappeared and everything in the garden was suddenly lovely. What point is there in seeing clearly what is wrong, and then not discussing it? It's a complete waste of time. I think you must bring things into the open. It's quite possible that, as a result, the other side will produce their arguments which hadn't occurred to you before, things which convince you you'd got hold of the wrong end of the stick. I don't believe in 'suffering in silence'.

"Many of us neither had nor have the background – you could even say the backbone – which you need to express your thoughts. On the other hand, some people would like to do so, but they don't know how to present a case. If you stutter or mumble in front of a big gathering, you always come off second best. They know this themselves and so they prefer to say nothing. This is one of the reasons why I was made the scapegoat so often. Although I also did my best to act for others, people used to say: it's only old Schockemöhle at it again. Many of the things attributed to me are simply not true. Of course I only acted when I was in agreement with the cause, where a change would also have been in my own interest. But in most cases I was acting as spokesman for a whole group. Why was I asked to put the case, rather than someone else? Perhaps I was the one with the biggest mouth – who knows? Perhaps I was the only one with enough selfconfidence to do it.

"Because of my whole background, my childhood, my education and my family, I've never been afraid of people in authority. I'd never address the Queen as 'Lizzie,' but neither would I sink through the floor with shyness if I were presented to her. To a large extent, this is due to the times we live in. We've all gone through great changes. The structure of society and our ways of thinking have altered completely in our lifetime. It's no use grumbling about whether it's good or bad. It can't be a bad thing

120

really if young people nowadays refuse to cheer obediently whenever they're told to. Now, of course, I'm no longer one of the generation for whom protest is a way of life. It's a phase everyone goes through.

"What has become of the protestors of the late sixties? They've become respectable family men, with a paunch and children and pension rights! I've never been a supporter of the extreme left in politics and with the money I earn these days, that would be ridiculous. I am what they call a capitalist –so what? That will never stop me from pointing out the things I consider bad, which can be altered, and which must be altered. As I said before, times have changed and I've no regrets about that. And if I've made a small contribution of my own even in the limited area of show jumping, I'm as proud of that as of a big win. I know then that it hasn't been in vain.

"Years ago, the cavalry school was the focal point of riding in Germany. At that time, in the social system of those days, this was right and proper, and our successes proved it. It would hardly have been possible any other way. It's all mixed up with simple things like the means of transport – how could a private citizen have afforded to send his horses hundreds of miles away by train, when the journey took several days? The European motorway network didn't exist then, nor were there transporters, not to mention aircraft. Who would have footed the bill at that time? How could first class competitions have been arranged? And if there isn't constant comparison, you can't tell how good you are. In sport, you need an audience in order to recognise your own faults.

"Today however, everything is different. In West Germany, as far as first class riders are concerned, the whole of riding is privately financed. For this reason, I don't agree with centralisation any longer. Since Gustav Rau's days, nothing has emerged from a central riding establishment of a standard high enough to compete at major international events.

"Riders are private citizens, not soldiers. The horse owners also are private citizens and not the army. They make available the money required for training, they sacrifice their time in order to discover such horses. But the organisation of equestrian sport is consuming a mint of money – money which actually belongs to us all. And no one in the private sector could spend money like that without going bankrupt fairly soon. Meanwhile, I've become an official myself; but I've often said and I say it again that I disapprove of this kind of work. The whole set-up is over-organised. It's organised for organisation's sake and not because it's of use to anyone. If I take on another twenty people tomorrow in my business, if I'm informed every day just how much steel mesh is in stock, where it is stored, and what is in transit, well and good. But if, as a result, my account is in the red at the end of the year, I'll have to stop and think where I've gone wrong.

"But suppose that for years on end I can cover the losses by subsidies from public funds, I quickly lose my feel for efficiency and responsibility. What's the good of computers stored with the most minute details? The cost involved is too high. And then they try to unload this cost on the horse owners and the riders, at least to some extent. The money must come from somewhere after all. If we riders and owners can't pay for it, it must come from the government – which means the taxpayers must stump up. It's all a kind of meaningless occupational therapy. Heaps of paper are fed into the computer, the results are stored in the basement, and if one fine day someone actually asks for some of these results, no one can find them on the shelves. First class riders nowadays are all dependent on something or other – on owners, on their own businesses, on the health of their horses – they all carry a certain risk – and that without any backing. On the contrary, the entry fees keep going up.

"This is where I see a fundamental difference between riding and other sports. A track athlete, a good one, would be provided with shoes, singlet and shorts. He is supported financially and when he gives up running, he is reimbursed for the time he has devoted to sport. He is also helped with his academic studies or his business training.

"I have to buy my own boots, my riding breeches, my jacket, the saddle, harness and of course the horse. And then along comes the organisation and tries to tell me how I'm to use them. Am I expected to approve? Should I accept orders meekly, just because the organisation says so? I don't agree with this and I never did. Nor do most of the other riders. I have no hesitation in describing our previous form of association as a dictatorship. It is still that to a large extent even today. For this reason, I shall go on working for changes and for new rules; there's a great deal still to do. When sport and business take up so much of your time, you can, of course, overlook things. For instance, there's a new rule calling for a big increase in the cost of entries and of stabling. And that just at a time when there are economic difficulties, when many things that ought to be tackled have to be postponed, and also at a time when wealthy patrons are not nearly so thick on the ground as they used to be, nor are they so free with their money. Indeed, their patronage could cease overnight.

"It would be much better if our officials would sit down in peace and quiet and try to work out ways of overcoming the present stagnation. It is highly unrealistic and also unbusinesslike simply to express the hope that because the country is mad about horses, all will be well again soon, that somehow or other someone will emerge who can be presented as the product of the association's management. I don't believe in such a product, in spite of my spell at Warendorf twenty years ago. I have become what I am today only through my own personal initiative and effort. And let them show me a single rider of world class in West Germany whose experience is different!

"I cannot share the thinking of the central training establishment's management at Warendorf. If they say that we can have financial support, we'll have to use it as we're told; if we refuse, we'll get nothing. This is a sad state of affairs. It's illogical, irresponsible even. It's precisely when you have to look after other people's money that you have to be more careful with it than if it were your own. And if that is what the laws demand, then they are bad laws and should be changed as quickly as possible. If I erect more buildings, I know beforehand that I shall also need more staff for their upkeep, more maintenance expenses, and therefore more money still next year.

"We don't need elementary training establishments for equestrian sports. What we need are instructors and most of all we need horses, which are not available at Warendorf. Nobody would dream of building a splendid race course with stables, practice rings and all the ancillaries, only to find they'd run out of money for horses. That's how Warendorf always seems to me; I don't understand it.

"It would be wrong to overstate the case and blame the officials and administration for all the mistakes. But I can't imagine that mature administrators are so short-sighted that they cannot see this frightful state of affairs, even when it is explained to them so clearly. I keep hearing that there is no money for horses, only for buildings. And so more and more buildings are going up. What do they expect us to ride at the Olympic Games or the World Championships? Houses? It must be made plain to those responsible that what we need are horses, not training sheds!

"This is a country where much is done for sport and I consider it to be a good investment, but even Germany can't afford to throw money away, because an unfortunate wording of the law says so. We have now started competing again with other countries; there's a lot of talk about the prestige that sport brings to the nation, with constant references to competition between the 'systems', when paying tribute to the achievements of sportsmen from East Germany. We're all in favour, but we don't want to carry the burden entirely by ourselves.

"All the good riders have their own training set up. In the last twenty years it has been proved that this decentralised system is right for our society and that it brings results. Hartwig Steenken, the present World Champion, owns a training establishment that cost something like 50,000 D-marks. The Warendorf establishment cost seven, eight or even more million D-marks. I'd like to ask the simple question: which of the two has produced more good horses in the course of the last few years? In sport as well as in business there must be something like cost effectiveness. One needn't look at it as they do in East Germany, where sportsmen, and whole areas of sport, suddenly disappear from international meetings simply because they aren't being successful. But with us too when no progress is made, there are inquiries and subsequent action. Something of the kind happens at the nomination of contestants for the Olympic Games, when a Federal Committee suddenly refuses to allow an association to let its athletes travel to Montreal or wherever, just because it is thought they don't stand a chance.

"I sometimes have the impression that it's our own fault we're in this position, simply because we are successful. By pointing to our successes which are all due to private initiative, we are refused the right to further support. Anyone who can think at all logically will find this simply laughable.

"I believe if things were put on a sensible basis, we could work well together. And incidentally this applies to other sports as well. I've said this often enough. Both Hartwig Steenken and I have proved that we're strong enough to reach the top even without Warendorf or a similar organisation. But we have also proved that it's impossible to prepare a team of boy or girl riders in a two or three weeks' training course. You can't make a master craftsman out of an apprentice in such a short space of time.

"One of my proposals would be that talented youngsters should be attached to the stables of experienced and successful riders. I know we ourselves are always busy, but such young people would have the opportunity to ride good horses with us, to receive instruction, and if they bring with them the determination to make the grade, they'll be able to benefit from their stay with us. They should also have at their disposal horses with which they stand a chance of sometimes winning prizes, or at least of being placed. There should be confidence in us that we can set these beginners on a promising career – always on condition that they themselves want it enough. Although this sounds rather hard for the young people concerned, I believe that their chances of success would in any event be higher than anything now offered at Warendorf.

"I don't see any other possibility, unless we alter our whole system and follow the example of the socialist countries where for months or years on end coaches and pupils are brought together and in this way achieve success. But one must of course rule that out for us. Dictatorships, absolute monarchies of the old style, and also socialist countries have it easier in many ways because of their centralised administration. We should be

125

glad that things are a bit more difficult for us.

"I don't want to be misunderstood. Of course I know that any organised activity also needs an administration. So do riders like us. We need an administration to issue regulations, to help and advise us in many fields. For this, one needs people and accommodation, but no stables and no indoor riding rings. What has been built in Warendorf during the last few years is completely superfluous in my opinion, no matter how brutal that may sound. As far as the sporting education of riders is concerned, these enormous buildings are wholly unnecessary.

"Of course it's difficult to alter this today, I know that as well as the next person. They've put up all this useless stuff, a vast amount of money has been spent – and is it all to be taken down again now? No one in his right senses could ask for that, although it could be argued it's the most sensible thing to do. We all have to live with our mistakes, but that doesn't mean we have to go on making them.

"It's exactly the same problem with the superb arena built in Riem for the Munich Olympics. This stadium cost many millions of D-marks and since the Games it has stood empty most of the time. And yet there was the example of the 1968 Mexico Games already there. They simply took a flat open space and put up stands round it, collapsible stands that could be taken down and used elsewhere later. The dressage at Schloss Nymphenburg was also arranged like this. It wouldn't have detracted in any way from the running of the Munich Games, and it would have saved a small fortune. In any event, the Nations' Cup was held in the Olympic stadium. If these removable stands had been used, they could have been offered afterwards for a small charge to the organisers of other meetings, and something useful for the future would have been achieved. It would have rendered a valuable service to competition organisers who find things very difficult today, it would have assisted the sport generally, and a cover organisation, a Warendorf, if you like, would have had a long term source of income from hiring them out. As things are, the sparrows and pigeons nest in peace on that wretched arena outside Munich and there's only a show once a year to disturb

126

their quiet lives. It's a pity about all that lovely money, though!"

Are Horses
Intelligent?

It has been said that Alwin Schockemöhle's way of training his horses was different from that of his rivals. His methods are used with a sensitive toughness (if that is possible), which certainly knows how far to go, but which demands the last ounce within those limits. Riders talking among themselves say that Alwin Schockemöhle can buy horses blindfold, and can "smell out" their class, even if they have never seen a fence before. This reputation presupposes an instinctive talent which has been developing ever since he was a toddler. His brother Werner, who is a lawyer, has written learned books on horsebreeding, which may well have been the results of their joint observations.

Be that as it may, there have been many discussions in recent years as to whether training for equestrian sports involves cruelty to the horse. Horst Stern's theories have been given much space. They aroused protests from riders but contained little of what might be called really sound scientific matter to argue about. Although a debate was very much desired, it did not take place. The point made by many riders and horselovers that one can hardly talk about cruelty in connection with such a pampered and cosseted creature as the horse is too frivolous to be taken altogether seriously.

Are horses stupid? Or to put it the other way round: are horses intelligent? Wilhelm Blendinger, who is considered to be one of the leading experts on the subject, has stated that: "The intelligence of horses scarcely differs from that of elephants. The prejudgment that calls a horse stupid arises from a misplaced comparison with the dog. A horse has much more in common with a cat than a dog, which is rightly classed as teachable. But teachability is an attribute of character, of an animal's willingness to

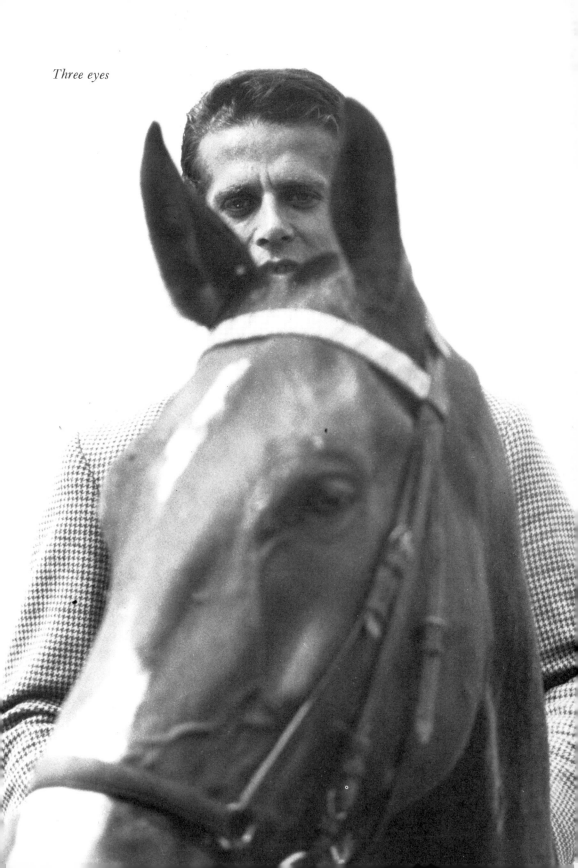

Three eyes

Horses from almost two decades: Extreme left: Alba, Dompfaff and Domspatz, at the outset of his career, mid to late 50's. Below left: Freiherr and Bacchus, 1963 – already becoming famous. Above right: Warwick Rex and Rex the Robber – the one reliable, the other beautiful – were the stars of the mid 70's

"*I can't switch myself off like a radio set. I keep thinking how I can improve something. I'm not upset about my so-called 'weak nerves'. I sometimes force myself to do things, but it isn't self-punishment. Because I enjoy the life I lead!*"

Faces of heroes, idols, friends, team members, rivals and partners from past decades. Below left: with his idol, Raimondo d'Inzeo. Above left: with his hero Fritz Thiedemann. Above centre: with the rest of the team, Hans Günter Winkler, Hermann Schridde and Kurt Jarasinski. Above right: with his friend and rival Nelson Pessoa. Below right: with his partner, Hartwig Steenken

There isn't a good rider anywhere in the world who doesn't sometimes come a cropper. (Old saying among riders)

learn, not of intelligence. Like the cat, the horse keeps his distance from man, he appears to be deliberately and intentionally unapproachable. If a horse shows an inclination towards a human being, it is to be considered more as condescension on his part, and is not to be compared with doglike devotion." The same author does not think much of research into animal behaviour which fails to do justice to the horse. "In no other species does one find so many individual characteristics in each specimen as in the horse, which in this respect is surpassed only by man."

Apparently the sceptic should exercise caution if he suspects that, in some degree, there is too much personification of animals. The question of an animal's memory may be illustrated by a brief aside on the subject of instinct. Teachability postulates incidentally a capacity to make use of what has been learnt. Does anyone seriously believe that a horse jumping a training oxer for the twentieth time does it with a view to perfecting its performance? A horse is hardly likely to understand why he is patted after a fault-free round, or punished after making several mistakes. "Halla laughed!" they used to say, which is absurd.

This raises the question of the meaning of the word intelligence, including human intelligence! Alwin Shockemöhle once said that his "most stupid" horse must have been Donald Rex, the horse with whom he achieved some spectacular successes. To which Blendinger replied: "Of course an intelligent creature cannot be influenced as easily as one with a simpler mentality!" And he added: "It's just the same with people."

Alwin Schockemöhle:
"In my opinion, horses know how to jump and they like jumping. This contradicts Horst Stern's theory which says the horse is, in the first instance, an animal that resorts to flight, and can only be forced to jump by using harsh methods. I don't want to give myself airs and lay down the law as to whether or not a horse gets particular pleasure from clearing obstacles, nor can I decide if it gets much pleasure from drawing a cart or a plough. I couldn't say for certain if a horse can feel anything like pleasure and enjoyment; so far, I've never seen one laugh or cry, and I don't discuss the subject with them either.

"But I can decide if a horse is ill or well. I can give

137

him the care he needs to keep him in good health, and I call a vet if I suspect there's something wrong. I've been dealing with horses now for well over twenty years, and exclusively with horses, not with other animals too, like Horst Stern. What does joy mean to an animal? When a healthy horse leaps over an obstacle of his own accord, is that joy? If so, I must certainly admit I've seen many horses jump for joy. I've known foals and unschooled two-year-olds who've jumped every fence in sight. Some cows do it too. I don't see any sense in condemning a whole sport just because someone has published a theory and insists it's the only valid one. What makes a young foal jump? Is it really practising for a time when it may need to run away from danger?

"I'm far too attached to horses ever to maltreat them. I consider animal protection societies are useful and sometimes even stronger steps should be taken if valuable horses are kept in a cold filthy stable and neglected so that they get worms and go sick.

"I school a promising horse as a coach trains a gifted sportsman. I try to make him more athletic, more supple, and slowly teach him how to jump better. And when my judgment tells me he has reached his limit, I don't push him any further. To return to the parallel with human beings: I know certain talented youngsters, children even, who burst into tears whenever they're sent for training which is much too strenuous for them. I believe my horses are much better off.

"Of course one must draw a distinction here too. There are admittedly many horses in show jumping who have no business to be there at all. They haven't the talent for it. It's the duty of the rider to recognise this. There should be much more discrimination. Horses who aren't jumpers and never will be shouldn't be there at all in the arena. Nor should the riders who refuse to acknowledge this is so, and who in spite of all the evidence try to force things to the limit. These people, I repeat, have no business to be in show jumping at all. I stick to my guns – in this sport, outstanding accomplishment is due not only to the rider's ability but also to that of the horse. And there are horses that can clear a jump of 1·80 metres (6ft) or even 2 metres (6ft 9ins) without using a whip or with much help from the rider.

138

"This doesn't mean, however, that accusations of cruelty to animals are not justified sometimes. There are riders who try to get more out of their horses than the animal can give. I'd go so far as to say that this is really a kind of unfair competition. In the main, it's the good riders who present good horses – horses for which they've paid a lot of money and trained with much patience, time and effort. Then someone turns up at a meeting with a badly prepared and perhaps untalented horse – a rider who hasn't put in any work at all, but who wants to achieve the same results by the use of force. This kind of thing turns the stomach of every decent horseman. In my opinion heavy fines should be imposed in such cases.

"Recently there has been a lot of discussion about cruelty in show jumping. It has been backed by photographs which show techniques that I personally consider both useless and stupid. Unfortunately, such photographs may put ideas into someone's head. The word 'aids' appears to me to be unacceptable to describe these techniques. They are not 'aids' but traps for the animal.

"Anyone who believes he can get better results by such means is simply stupid; he understands little of the sport and nothing at all of horses. I maintain that dirty tricks like these defeat their own object. It may perhaps be possible to obtain better results on two or three occasions than if it had been left to the horse naturally, but the effect is short-lived. Afterwards the horse will be even worse than before; and which thinking person will ignore all the money a horse costs just for the sake of a couple of wins?

"Are horses intelligent? That's a big question. Surely the answer is no, if measured by the same standards as human intelligence. The circus trick with the horse that can count has probably been around as long as man and horse have been together. Intelligence surely means being able to use past experience positively. 'Experience' may not be quite the right word, though. Perhaps it would be more accurate to say that during training you can guide the horse's instinct in certain directions. Of course the horse feels the difference between jumping in front of a capacity audience in the stadium and the peacefulness of the training ground. He takes in the noise, the flickering movement – after all he has eyes and ears, perhaps he even senses the nervousness which no rider is quite free from. Here I should like to go back to my favourite grey, Rex the Robber. If there is such a thing as intelligence in a horse, then he has it in abundance. But it's more a disadvantage than an asset. Robber let's himself be side-tracked, he's difficult to bring under control. Against this is the other example of Donald Rex, the bay gelding. With him I had the finest possible series of successes. But this, I believe, was due to the fact that Donald was what in human terms we would call a simple soul. In a word, he wasn't very bright. Donald, however, wouldn't let himself be diverted by anything – he did exactly what was asked of him. If you'd have let off a bomb next to him, he wouldn't have flinched.

"Of course the attitude of a rider to his 'sports equipment' is totally different from that of a gymnast to his apparatus or a footballer to his football. This has nothing to do with the fact that the horse costs more. The gymnast has his apparatus placed in position, the football is blown up. Where a car is concerned, you know its horsepower and acceleration. No, the relationship with a horse is not comparable with any of these. Here is a living creature that comes to meet you, who wants to be petted, who must be fed and kept clean, who can also be angry, bad tempered, shy – a bicycle can't get nasty with its owner.

"No two horses are alike. In this respect they have something human about them. There are some horses, I can tell at once, that take to me immediately. Others, I know, must get used to my person slowly. And there are others still where there's constant conflict which nothing will put right, try as you may. As a rider and horseowner, you are bound to subordinate your personal feelings but there really is something like sympathy and antipathy. Properly speaking, such feelings only apply to human relationships, but during the many years I've been concerned with horses, I know it's quite spontaneous. You may be totally unaware of it, then suddenly it's there. Love is probably pitching it too high – affection is a better word.

"It should be said too that in any other sport, equipment can be changed at will. With a horse you can't do this. First of all you must find a new horse. Then you must buy it and start training it all over again.

"I've had many different feelings towards the many different horses I've ridden, but there's always one for which I have a special liking. It may be the way he comes towards me as I enter the stable, or I like the colour. Successes too play a part, of course, but they're not nearly as decisive as might be assumed. There are horses that get away with a lot more cheek. They may bite and scuffle, and I just give them a lump of sugar, stroke them and soothe them down, and pretend that all's well. With others I take umbrage and get upset over trifles, and I'm much more severe in my treatment of them. It's a bit like parents and children sometimes. One child is allowed to get away with murder, because he's the favourite, and the others are treated much more strictly. This is unjust, of course, as every parent would admit, and yet on the next occasion they do exactly the same thing. It's human nature. Looked at in this way, I too approach my horses with something like human feelings.

"But one of the human feelings I never extend to any horse is disappointment, for here the horse really is no more than a so-called 'piece of equipment'. You can be disappointed in a human being who has, say, let you down or swindled you. With a horse, I can no more be disappointed than any other sportsman with his gear. I can swear at a horse that suddenly stops or throws me – I may call it a bugger or something of the kind – but surely this is identical with a cyclist's reaction after his third puncture.

"The explanation for this attitude is comparatively simple. Anyone who has spent as much time in the saddle as I have, knows that for such a thing to happen there must have been some previous mistake on my part, something I had failed to foresee. Only I can be disappointed if the horse throws me in the mud, out of sheer bad temper or spite – if he seems to be having his own back, I am tempted to react: 'I'll show him!' But this is all nonsense. Once again it's overrating animal intelligence. Spite and revenge are much too human.

"No. As far as mistakes go, I take a realistic view. By evening at the latest, when you're counting your bruises, you realise what were the causes that led to the mistake. Perhaps I had misjudged the moment of take off, perhaps the ground was so soft that the horse slipped and couldn't get a firm hold. Often enough the reason lies in the jump made two or three back – the falling pole then is the cause of what happened later, a kind of chain reaction. Of course it is always possible that the horse was not on form, but that also was my mistake, something I should have recognised earlier. Or I may have actually noticed it, but let it go, hoping everything would be all right after all. It could be that the horse wasn't quite ready for this particular trial. This brings me to one of the most important qualities a rider needs. He must know how to wait. He needs patience. The decision, the responsibility is that of the rider and not the horse. And disappointment can only properly apply to the person responsible.

"Mistakes can also arise from being overambitious. No one will ever succeed without ambition, but it must be in the right degree. Too much is as bad as too little. When a rider is young, he can't judge this for himself. Only good coaches and good friends can put him right; they and the experience that comes with the years. I know that even for the World and the European Championships there are young riders who enter horses and who shouldn't be there at all. Of course it isn't easy to bring it home to these youngsters that they'd be better advised to wait a few years. As a teenager I too said: 'They want me out of the way.' I made the same mistake too. I wanted my chance at any price and as a result I often came a cropper. You hope for a miracle, and when it doesn't happen, you believe the whole world is conspiring against you. You have to go through this phase.

"I know that twenty years ago I often wanted to force the pace. I also know that sometimes I had incredible luck when a horse's performance was far beyond anything I could reasonably have expected. I know now that I made errors then which I wouldn't repeat today. But I know equally well that if I hadn't had such luck at that time, I'd have quickly given up riding altogether in the major events. Strangely enough, it isn't the defeats that spur you on but much more the wins. Once you've beaten the rest of the field, it becomes an incentive to repeat your success, and you can't understand why it has to stop some time or other. If you suddenly find you've slipped to the bottom of the table, you cling to your one victory – a hope which has destroyed many riders – and indeed many other sportsmen. At this point, you try to force things – more intensive training, perhaps even doping – but nothing helps.

"After all these years, I know before I leave for a meeting whether or not I'm going to be successful. Why on earth should a horse who hasn't displayed good form during training suddenly be expected to give a fault-free performance in the arena? I've long since given up hoping for such miracles. Indeed, at the Olympic Games, the World or European Championships, such a thing couldn't happen, because the competitors there are always prepared to peak condition; one can't just muddle through somehow or other as may have been possible at a small event where the other mounts were even worse than one's own. These days, I'd rather leave a horse like that at home and take along some of the younger ones.

"It has been said that first class riders could get a good placing even on a cow. I have my doubts. . . . A first class rider always has a certain chance of success even on a horse which isn't quite top class. But first of all, this is really something of a gamble, and secondly it couldn't happen at one of the big meetings. At major prize events, which in Germany are often more testing than many international competitions, such a pair could never in fact be successful. When a 'Grand Master' like Hans Heinrich Brinkmann constructs a really difficult course, there's no such thing as luck. You can only win then if you're good. By this I mean when both are good, horse and rider too."

Not Quite Perfect:

Here is another odd fact about sport. There are long tables of results where the winners for decades past are recorded, nothing but names, which say nothing at all about the contest that brought their owners to distinction; nothing about how hard a tussle it was, nor whether those who were beaten were of world class. The much coveted mention in these lists says nothing either of the many years of hard work which went before, nothing about good luck or bad – only the names and nothing else. There are world record holders who in their own field of sport dominated a whole epoch, but who never won a major championship. Others, on the contrary, of whom hardly anyone had heard before or after the event, remain inscribed there for ever.

Hans Günter Winkler once said: "You're an Olympic gold medallist for all time. You're only World Champion until the next World Championship." He should know – he's won them both. There are degrees of prestige between the Olympic Games and the World and European Championships, but it's the contest itself that demands the same one hundred per cent application every time.

Alwin Schockemöhle:

"You're an Olympic gold medallist only till the next Games, and probably someone else will win then. I don't make any distinction between the major titles there are to be won. You can argue about the rules that govern the results. But the varying degrees of importance ascribed to the winners are, in my opinion, due solely to the mass media.

"Naturally I can see that an Olympic victory will be rated more highly than the others. But for me, this is mainly because of the way the competition is conducted. At the World Championships, where the finalists must

144

exchange horses, the difficulties increase all the time. These are due primarily to the mere fact of having to ride a strange horse. The course itself is not particularly taxing even by the standards of national trials, but on those occasions you're always riding a horse of your own. I don't think this is an ideal formula.

"Of course I have my own special reasons for objecting here. At the World Championship finals, Donald Rex was far and away the best horse, but that didn't do me much good; my rivals were more successful with my well-trained horse than I was with theirs. All your hard work has been for the benefit of the others. Of course it is obvious that to reach the final four I need my good horse to start with, but the top four are always first class riders in any event. All the same, you wonder if it wouldn't have been more in your own interest to prepare a horse less well, so that your opponents had a few more difficulties to contend with. But wouldn't this be unfair? The others in fact do it unconsciously. Is it unfair if I do it deliberately?

"At the World Championships, the differences in the methods of preparing the horses are much more apparent than at the Olympic Games. The riders of the world may argue about this for days on end without coming to any rational conclusion. Is the German way the right one? Or are the British, the Americans or the Italians right? Of course I consider my methods are right, and for me they are. But there are wide differences of opinion.

"We in Germany try to achieve absolute perfection in a horse. No matter what we ask a horse to perform later, the training we give him is dressage based. We want to have the horse always under perfect control; we want one hundred per cent obedience. The horse should react to the slightest aid, he must be positioned exactly where we want him to be to the nearest centimetre. That is why our horses are always so sought after abroad. Everyone prefers an obedient horse.

"Riders abroad have wholly different attitudes. They try to come to a compromise with the horse. They tend to adapt themselves much more to the animal's mood of the moment. If because of this they get into trouble in the arena, they have to improvise. They must rely much more on feel, and correct things as they go. All these are things, incidents, we try to avoid beforehand. Critics accuse us of aiming at perfection, but I consider that is right. Our way of riding may give the impression we're riding with the handbrake on, whereas the others give dazzling performances with long galloping strides. All the same, we've often proved that we can move fast too – but it's when we want to, and not when the horse feels like it.

"This is due purely and simply to the system we use, but it's one that neither the Americans nor the Italians favour. If the horse wants to run, they let it, and only try to guide it in the direction of the fences. If they remain fault free – and they often do, I admit – they've been very lucky. But you can't really call it a system. To some extent our method has a lot to do with the German character. We like things to be perfect. But in addition, I consider this to be the beginning and end of equestrianism. We have good arguments for our system; they can be seen in all the results tables of the Olympic Games. No other team has won so many medals. We try to avoid excessive risks, so that the horse is always under control. But this is a task which begins months or even years before, so a defeat is much more painful for us than for someone whose effort has been confined to a few weeks' preparation.

"You can compare it with driving a car. Before I set off, I must know that the brakes are working and that the carburettor is adjusted correctly. It's a question of safety, even if people do come and tell us that we're treating live horses as if they were lifeless cars. What we do is, in fact, for the safety of the horses as well; that is why we train them so thoroughly, so that we know what kind of performance we can expect from them.

"This doesn't mean that we think the Germans have staked a claim to gold medals as of right. After all, some twenty nations send their best riders to the Olympic Games – why shouldn't they be lucky sometimes? Or to put it the other way round: why shouldn't we be unlucky sometimes? But when all is said and done, the long list of German successes in the Nations' Cup is something that can't be explained away very easily."

The aim of this book has been to describe how one man – Alwin Schockemöhle – contributed to such successes; to provide some insight into his ideas and attitudes and the secrets of his riding techniques. It only remains to add a few highlights, a touch of colour here and there, which may help to complete the portrait.

A GLUTTON FOR PUNISHMENT?

"I once hurt myself badly at the European Championships in Lucerne. It was at the last jump. I only recovered consciousness two days later – otherwise I hardly remember anything of what happened. The doctor told me I must stay in bed for three weeks. One week later I was riding in Aachen. It was idiotic – a young man's mistake. As a result, I had to withdraw for quite a long period. But you can't call that being a glutton for punishment. I used to be very ambitious. I still am. The whole business of show jumping is something I find exciting. Without enthusiasm, it simply isn't possible to succeed. Too much is better than too little. It gives me pleasure just to go riding on Sunday afternoons, or even just working with horses. Would it be better if I sat in an armchair instead, watching a film? Or reading the paper? Or eating cake? I don't mind if others prefer these things, but I arrange my life differently. It must be my activity not that of other people. In every sport there comes a time when you say to yourself: this is the end, I'm no good any more, why do I go on punishing myself? That's the inner demon you have to overcome. But I don't complain. No one has forced me to do all this. I wouldn't allow anyone to force me. I forced myself, but I didn't really see myself as a glutton for punishment. Because I actually enjoyed the life I led – that's the main reason!"

CHILDHOOD:

"As a child, whenever there was anything to do with horses happening on the cindertrack in Emsland, I was there. Does any boy think of the future at that stage? A week is about all you can envisage, a year is eternity. My daughter is interested in horses, my sons not at all. I don't want to influence them. They must please themselves, although of course they are bound to be influenced

147

to some extent by their home background. And this background includes horses in a big way. My childhood didn't do me any harm."

MAJOR WINS:

"At the moment of success, you don't realise what's happening. You're pleased with the tumultuous applause, people congratulate you, the newspapers are full of it. Before you've time to think properly, days or even weeks have elapsed. By then there may have been other events, other results perhaps that weren't so good. Then you come down to earth very quickly. Big wins are only big at the actual moment of achievement. You forget them quickly. This isn't true only of the public – it goes for me too."

MAJOR DISAPPOINTMENTS:

"With disappointments, it's very much the same as with successes, and mainly for much the same reasons. In Tokyo, 1964, I was really disappointed. In Mexico four years later, I was as pleased with the bronze as if it had been a gold, because I could be satisfied with my own performance. That's extremely important. If you're satisfied with yourself, it's as good as a win. You know you've done everything correctly, you needn't reproach yourself and that's enough. In 1972 in Munich, the situation was quite different. I had counted on having Donald Rex and Wimpel, two first class horses, whom I thought I could rely on for at least another three years. And then both had to be withdrawn within a few days of each other. At first of course I hoped I could get by with another horse, but I quickly realised it wasn't possible, so I withdrew from the qualifying events. By withdrawing early it wasn't so disappointing being an ordinary spectator at the Games – I'd had enough time to get used to the idea – although it was hard, of course, particularly in your own country, being forced to watch. But it wouldn't have been honest or fair to try to muddle through the qualifying events on some mediocre horse. As I said, I had time to get used to the idea. So it wasn't a disappointment any longer."

148

THE SOCIAL SYSTEM:

"All I possessed twenty years ago was my riding ability. Goodnatured cynics said I'd been blessed with a highly gifted backside. If you want to be stuffy, you could say that that's not very much for anyone intelligent. People can say what they like. I know today that I can afford to be a perfectly 'clean' amateur. And it isn't entirely due to my bottom, but also to my head. At a decisive moment, I cut myself off from a large part of my past and made a completely fresh start. This could also have gone wrong, but that didn't weigh with me for one moment. I no longer ride for a living, I live to be able to ride. This is probably the most convincing proof of my claim to be considered as an amateur.

"A split personality doesn't come into it. I must first build up something which enables me to earn a living, before I can assert my amateur status with a clear conscience! This is where the social system is wrong. If by chance I had been born in East Germany and, again by chance, I had been successful, I might today be the proud owner of a flat and a car. I'm pretty sure that that system wouldn't have pleased me either. There's too much theorising about such things for my liking. I don't know which is the middle course one ought to steer. But I do know that riding shouldn't be left to anyone who does it as a hobby, it's much too serious for that!"

FRIENDS:

"There are many people I get on with very well. I don't know if they can all be counted as my friends. A friend in need is a friend indeed, as the saying goes. In this respect I've been fairly lucky so far. I've never been in really dire straits either in sport or in business, so I've never had to call on friends for help. I've never had to borrow money so far, so I can't say if many of my friendships would have survived such a test. But friendship is not only making demands on people but when they make demands on you. You need two people for friendship, it's not a one-sided affair. In show jumping I've been through so many highs and lows. You don't always need extravagant expressions of friendship. If a day came

149

when I really was in trouble, I believe I'd find quite a few people whom I could describe as friends."

WORK:

"I was a farmer, and I became a businessman and a manufacturer. The land is let now; business absorbs all my time. I don't much like the term 'Manager'."

SPORT:

"Even if I'd grown up in quite a different milieu I'd always have liked to have something to do with sport. I don't know why; it's something in my make-up. It's difficult to explain. I like competition, I like pitting myself against others. I could never see myself as a person who goes to the office every morning and comes home at night to sit in front of the telly. My association with equestrian sports arose quite naturally from my home background. And there's one thing more I'm certain of: no matter what sport I'd have taken up, I'd have reached the top."

MONEY:

"As a young man I had no money. Today I have some. In my opinion, you can never say you've enough money. It's a means of fulfilling one's desires, and there's always something else you want. Anyone who says he has no desires must be a poor specimen. I enjoy work but perhaps I have a gift for recognising if it's going to be worthwhile or not. If the latter, I prefer to drop it and turn to something else. But as I never sit around doing nothing and, on the other hand, concentrate on what is rewarding, I probably earn more than people who waste their time. For me, money is a means of buying the things that give me pleasure – riding is certainly one of them. Money allows me to live in the style I like."

DESIRES:

"We all have our dreams and wishes, but I for instance, would never want to live on a South Sea island. Maybe

150

one day I'd like to work less, take things a little easier. But this will happen of its own accord. I'm getting older, more reasonable. One day, I should like not to have to travel so much. On the other hand mine is an exciting life and that adds to my satisfaction. This is how I wanted it and now I have it. If I examine my life closely, I'm really very contented. Yes indeed, the way I live now suits me down to the ground!"

Gold in Bromont

Bromont had only been in existence a dozen years or so when they built a stadium there that made a mockery of all the groans about the ever-increasing scale of the Olympic Games. Probably no other modern stadium in the world so closely resembles the ancient arena in the sacred grove of Olympia. Apparently a very wealthy man had made available the money to bring the riding competitions here. He really put Bromont on the map. In North America such a thing is still possible.

The natural slope of the ground, which is wooded at the top, forms the grandstand of this stadium. At the foot of the slope lies the big field which is the arena itself. Two smaller stands, for reporters and for guests of honour, were built on the opposite side of the arena. They seem strangely at odds with the rest of the scene.

It was one of those sultry mornings when you can tell there's thunder in the air as soon as you wake. During the first round, as more than forty riders fought their way with varying degrees of success through the forest of obstacles (and while early hopes such as those of the young and confident Paul Schockemöhle were shattered), the inky clouds drifted slowly across the sky, and the eerie twilight of silence was broken only by the applause of the spectators and the clatter of falling poles.

Alwin Schockemöhle was the only rider who had not contributed to the clatter, and as a reward for his clear round he was much applauded. He had completed this course, which included no less than sixteen oxers, without a fault. His gelding Warwick Rex had flown over them as easily as if he had been at home in his own practice ring and not at the Olympic Games. The accomplishment so far did not mean much; only that because of it, Alwin Schockemöhle was assured of at least

The most successful team in the Olympic jumping events: Gold and silver for Alwin Schockemöhle and Warwick Rex

Alwin Schockemöhle and Sönke Sönksen (above left) in the grandstand. The enforced retirement of the quiet Sönke Sönksen in Alwin Schockemöhle's favour gave rise to much discussion. Below left: conversation between team-mates, Alwin Schockemöhle and Hans Günter Winkler, who was overshadowed by the former both in Bromont and in Montreal
Above right: Homage to the winners in Bromont: left to right – Michel Vaillancourt (Canada – silver), Alwin Schockemöhle, and François Mathy (Belgium – bronze)

*The bay gelding Warwick Rex leaps the fences with an ease
that places him in a class above all other competitors*

*Grand Finale of the Montreal Olympic
Games – the final of the Nations' Cup.
Alwin Schockemöhle on Warwick Rex, but
this time there was only a silver for him
and the German team. Below: Germans,
French and Belgians on the winners' podium
From left to right: Paul Schockemöhle, Hans
Günter Winkler, Alwin Schockemöhle,
Sönke Sönksen. The French riders: Hubert
Parot, Marcel Rozier, Marc Roguet and
Michel Roche. Beside them, the four
Belgian riders*

Gold and Silver – Alwin Schockemöhle

twentieth place in the individual jumping event at the Games, since twenty riders would qualify for the second round in the afternoon.

It could have been looked on either as a disadvantage or an advantage that Alwin Schockemöhle was due to ride last. It might have made him happy, as it's useful perhaps to know how one's rivals have fared in the arena. On the other hand, the two hour wait is nerve-racking. He hardly spoke to anyone. he had a bite to eat without noticing what it was, he went back to the collecting ring and heard the announcements blaring over the loud-speaker.

At the very beginning of this round the Mexican Carlos Aguirre and the Puerto Rican rider with the German surname, Juan Rieckehoff, both fell heavily and retired. Of the so-called twenty best in this round, fourteen finished with more than ten faults. With the exception of the Belgian, Francois Mathy on Gay Luron, every rider in the second round put up a worse performance than in the first one. This is an unusual occurrence. And no one can develop such perfect self-confidence that waiting doesn't affect him.

In the meantime, the sky had turned blue black, the first flash of lightning was expected at any moment and the rain threatened to come pouring down, which would make the going so soft as to destroy the chances of the last rider.

Alwin Schockemöhle had not yet been called. As the rider before him left the arena, Schockemöhle pushed past him into the stadium. Two officials tried to stop him. He simply didn't see them. They jumped aside in alarm as Warwick Rex made straight for the entrance gate. Later the rider admitted: "I was only afraid the rain would start. Warwick Rex isn't easily frightened by lightning, but how could I tell what his reaction would have been if a really heavy thunderstorm had suddenly broken loose? I didn't even hear what they were saying over the loudspeakers any more. My only thought was to get into the arena before the cloudburst."

The bay gelding soared over the forest of obstacles with an ease that placed him in a class above all his rivals. In the middle of the round someone cheered and was immediately hushed. Friends turned their heads, they

161

couldn't bear to look. No one could believe that here where the best riders in the world had collected penalty after penalty, Alwin Schockemöhle on Warwick Rex would remain in the clear. Someone had called to him as he entered the arena that he could afford to knock over a couple of fences and still win the gold, but he hadn't heard.

As he took off for the final jump, the triple combination, Alwin Schockemöhle was already "home and dry". With the middle element behind him, it was all but over, and when he finally cleared the last fence, he had proved himself the most outstanding Olympic gold medallist for show jumping there had ever been.

Even before he reached the finishing line, the rider whipped off his cap – a flourish of triumph – not so much a victory over his opponents as over this course. It was as if he had mastered a living creature. It was a kind of salute, a movement one sees during a football match, when the goalkeeper runs half round the pitch like a madman and jumps into the air, raising his fists to the heavens. A horseman doffs his cap. There's homage in this gesture too. He had waited twenty years for that moment.

There was no one that day who would not have acknowledged Alwin Schockemöhle as the best show jumper in the world. They all came to congratulate him or at least to give him a pat on the back. No sooner had he finished the course and reached the collecting ring behind the huge scoreboard when the storm broke. The jump-off between the Canadian Michael Vaillancourt, the Belgian François Mathy and the young British rider Debbie Johnsey had to take place in pouring rain. That was the order in which they finished for the remaining places.

Behind the scenes hardly anyone noticed the rain. People came to see him, including Hans Günter Winkler who had been fêted in the same way twenty years before, the American Frank Chapot, an honourable fighter and rival, the Italian Raimondo d'Inzeo, once Schockemöhle's greatest idol and now beaten by his "fan". There were also those who pushed in, anxious for some reason or other to be photographed with him, or to have such a picture published. Friends came, and officials too, of course.

162

One of them slapped him on the back: "Thank goodness my Sauerland skull was thicker than your Oldenburg one!" These two German regions are somewhat notorious for obstinacy. The speaker, the president of the German Riders Association, was the first to refer to the events of the previous weeks, which had not always been exactly pleasant.

One must go back to a meeting on October 14th 1975 in Mühlen, called for the purpose of laying down a qualifying system for the choice of German show jumpers to take part in the Montreal Olympics. Six riders and horses were accorded the status of belonging to the Olympic cadre: Fritz Ligges with Genius, Hartwig Steenken with Kosmos, Alwin Schockemöhle with Warwick Rex, Hendrik Snoek with Gaylord, Sönke Sönksen with Kwept, and Hans Günter Winkler with Torphy. At that time, Gerd Wiltfang was still under investigation on a charge of cruelty, which was later quashed, and this meant that he too was included later. Paul Schockemöhle was asked to explain certain statements he had made during the preceding months, before he was accepted as well. The Mannheim and Balve meetings were designated as preliminary trials. The qualifying events, it was agreed, should be firstly the Aachen and Verden meetings, and later on, Cologne.

Every four years, these Olympic selections become a bone of contention among the riding fraternity with unpleasant regularity. The real reason is ironically due to an encouraging state of affairs. In no other country are there more first class riders fit to represent their country than in West Germany, and they all believe they stand a good chance of competing at the Olympic Games. When the team of Alwin Schockemöhle, Hans Günter Winkler and Fritz Thiedemann won the gold medal at the Rome Olympics in 1960, a word from an influential person was sufficient to decide who should ride for West Germany. Nowadays it no longer works like that, in the first place because a little democracy has crept into the procedure, and secondly because of the greater number of riders.

This tricky business of selection which cuts across families and sours friendships cannot be compared with similar processes in other branches of sport. If a hundred metre sprinter has won her place in the Olympic team, she or her coach are the only ones to decide the best programme for the preceding weeks. She will rest and train, eat the right food and if required, take part in one or other of the suitable competitions. The preparation of a horse for competitive events cannot be compared with that of a human being.

Fritz Thiedemann once said that a horse has only a certain number of jumps in him, and once these have been used up, that's the end. Of course this is only a theory, but assuming it is based on fact, it can be that a horse is well ahead of all others during the selection tests, but when it comes to the real thing, he can't make the grade. Even if one doesn't believe in this theory, it still means that the riders concerned have to present their horses in peak form twice within a matter of a few months, which is hardly feasible. During the qualifying trials, the horses must be seen to be fit, but not too fit; and if you're unlucky when there are so many equally good riders, you may easily end up bottom of the list. As someone once said: "You can qualify yourself to death." There is no satisfactory solution. Neither does there exist a universally respected dictator who simply says: "You, you and you!" and that's the end of the argument. This is readily understandable. Who would be willing to accept so much personal responsibility?

The three months leading up to Alwin Schockemöhle's Olympic victory were anything but a peaceful preparation for the severest test of one's life. Seldom has the concept of sport as a splendid but wholly unimportant affair been made nonsense of so utterly as in this particular case.

The timetable started at the beginning of May, with the preliminary trials in Mannheim, where there was much talk of Gerd Wiltfang's fine successes; but Mannheim was not obligatory. About that time, the American showjumpers had arrived in Germany to complete their final preparations. Berthalan de Nemethy, who has prepared the U.S. riders for their big events for the last twenty years – the man whose own training was at the famous Hanover Cavalry School – who looks so like a "gentleman-rider" that it's almost a caricature – de Nemethy declared outright that the Germans were favourites for the Games: "Because they are quite simply the best there are, and because I'd like my strongest

164

rivals to be looked on as the favourites!"

A week later was the Balve meeting, again only a preparatory trial, where Paul Schockemöhle, Hendrik Snoek and the World Champion Hartwig Steenken presented their horses. The "Grand Master" Hans Heinrich Brinckmann, who also holds the position of official trainer, said that in his opinion, the horses should be schooled slowly to Olympic standards. His course on that occasion compelled a large number of riders to retire.

Alwin Schockemöhle reported that his horses were sick. Hans Günter Winkler said the same about Torphy. For the first time there was a certain mistrust in the air. And an independent team of medical experts was asked to decide whether these horses were in fact unfit.

The possibility of such incidents and the need for their investigation had been anticipated, and procedure had been laid down accordingly in November 1975. Alwin Schockemöhle decided not to enter Warwick Rex for the C.S.I.O. meeting in Aachen. The reason for this late decision was that the gelding had been suffering from a virus infection for the last few weeks. It was also confirmed that Winkler's Torphy now had a hoof infection. Both riders, however, were assured that they would have an opportunity of competing for a place in the Olympic team at Verden and also at Cologne.

To sum up so far: with the Olympic jumping events at Bromont only two months away, neither of these horses had been presented at any of the so-called qualifying events.

It was at Aachen that hard words were spoken for the first time. Hartwig Steenken, who had ridden Gladstone to victory in the German Championship, was clearly referring to Schockemöhle and Winkler when he declared that the riders who were actually competing at Aachen would be more suitable for the Montreal team than the two who were absent. Winkler appeared indifferent, and said he would forgo an Olympic place if he hadn't a suitable horse. And Alwin Schockemöhle stated: "I certainly don't have to go. Warwick Rex is only up to Olympic standards when he's really on form."

Premature resignation? Or taking umbrage? No one then in the Soers arena at Aachen was looking forward with particular enthusiasm to the Montreal Olympics. It was said that Hendrik Snoek and Fritz Ligges had already ridden their horses out of the short list. Winkler's rivals were demanding that his horse Torphy, who was slowly returning to peak form, should be submitted to a doping test.

Of course nothing came of it except bitterness and bad blood. Two of the supposedly safe nominations, Paul Schockemöhle and Hartwig Steenken were insisting on confirmation for the individual event as well as the Nations' Cup. Neither of them was willing to go to Canada for the team event, and only as fourth man for the individual competition.

At this point, it should be mentioned that Henk Nooren, the 21-year-old Dutchman who has looked up to Hans Günter Winkler as his idol for many years, and whose riding style is based on that of his hero, when asked who would be the next Olympic winner said immediately: "Alwin Schockemöhle on Warwick Rex."

In Verden, at last, there was to be a meeting with all the eight "mentioned" present. For the first time, Hartwig Steenken found it possible to speak without acrimony. He really didn't want to go to Montreal any longer. Alwin Schockemöhle declared his willingness to go; indeed, he felt he had to, although the date didn't fit in with the rest of his training programme. When the Verden meeting was over, the decision seemed more difficult than ever. Snoek on Gaylord had come out ahead of Winkler riding Torphy. Alwin Schockemöhle had left Warwick Rex at home. His brother Paul had done the same with Talisman, and so had Steenken with Kosmos. During the interval, between the first and second rounds of the major competition, they tossed up. Is this the way to decide who is to compete at the Olympic Games?

During the last week in May the World Champion Hartwig Steenken definitely stated that he would not take any further part in the selection. His horse Kosmos was sick and his two other "possibles" were too young. He didn't even feel like going to Montreal as a spectator. He would rather go to Belgrade and watch the European football championship match a week or two before.

Hartwig Steenken, the World Champion, who had for years been one of the finest riders in the world, wouldn't

166

be present at the Olympic Games. And furthermore, in all probability, neither would the most successful jumper of the previous year, Alwin Schockemöhle, the European Champion. Nor even the man who had won five Olympic gold medals, Hans Günter Winkler – a whole team in themselves more famous than all the "rest of the world" put together.

Hartwig Steenken observed: "What's the good of going when I don't stand a chance?" Another trial jump in Verden gave Sönke Sönksen on Kwept the lead over Paul Schockemöhle on Talisman, Gerd Wiltfang on Davos, Winkler on Torphy and Alwin Schockemöhle on Warwick Rex. This is how things stood. The only firm recommendation so far was Torphy with Winkler riding. And of course the quiet Sönke Sönksen, who had hardly been in the running hitherto. Torphy and Warwick Rex, with their riders were summoned to compete in Cologne. The trials there were to take place in the middle of June, five weeks before the Games were due to start.

Perhaps this is a good place to mention the panel which was to nominate the show jumping competitors. It had before it a heap of tables and figures, with cross-referenced comparisons of questionable value. Even those who hadn't much time for the panel at all were forced to admit that it was difficult if not downright impossible to arrive at conclusions acceptable to everyone. Ten days before the Cologne Trials, the panel made their first two nominations, Paul Schockemöhle and Sönke Sönksen. These were the first visible results of the qualifying system. One doubts if anyone was really happy with it.

Before the final trials in Cologne, there was the traditional meeting in the park of the castle at Wiesbaden-Biebrich. At last Warwick Rex, the bay gelding, showed he was in satisfactory shape, which had a calming and relaxing effect on Alwin Schockemöhle, with Cologne so close. In riding competitions, nervousness and restlessness always communicate themselves to the horse.

The results of the Cologne Trials surely have no equal in history. There was a placing, but no outright winner. This is how the outcome was announced: Hans Günter Winkler on Torphy, had had one pole down, ahead of Alwin Schockemöhle on Warwick Rex, who had two poles down and a $\frac{3}{4}$ time penalty, and of Gerd Wiltfang riding Davos with $18\frac{1}{4}$ faults altogether. There were no other competitors. The two rounds had consisted of 28 jumps (15 plus 13).

Fritz Ligges, who had also been invited to complete for an Olympic place said: "No, thanks!" and withdrew. As Alwin Schockemöhle quitted this farce of a trial, he said he thought that this "ghost arena" had been designed to present much greater difficulties than anything seen in the earlier elimination events. Winkler gave his opinion that people were trying to "murder" him and the other competitors.

In addition to the two riders already confirmed, the panel now nominated Alwin Schockemöhle and Hans Günter Winkler, with Hendrik Snoek as fifth. Gradually it dawned on the bewildered Alwin Schockemöhle that, according to Steenken, Ligges and Snoek, Sönksen's Kwept should be entered for the individual event, together with Torphy and Talisman, to be ridden by Winkler and Paul Schockemöhle respectively. He, Alwin Schockemöhle, was out. This was confirmed three weeks later by the panel, but admittedly with a proviso that another decision might be possible at the last minute.

At this, Alwin Schockemöhle declared at once that he would withdraw and not go to Montreal. "If Warwick Rex and I aren't good enough for the individual event, we're not good enough for the Nations' Cup either." Negotiations went on for hours between the obstinate President who came from the Sauerland, and the equally obstinate show jumper from Oldenburg. It was Alwin's brother Werner, the lawyer and eminent horse expert, who finally talked him into changing his mind. "I'm doing it for the sake of the others," said Alwin Schockemöhle. That was one week before the departure.

Two days before the individual event in Bromont, the panel decided that Warwick Rex was in cracking form and must therefore compete. It was made clear to Sönke Sönksen that he must step down – at which the latter called it "a dirty trick" and said he would go home. Sönksen, who comes from Holstein, accused Alwin Schockemöhle of "pushing him out of the ring", which Schockemöhle refuted. All he had done was to bring his horse to peak form. In his opinion, Kwept with Sönksen riding him seemed to be second only to Warwick

168

during training.

This discussion took place only about forty hours before the start. The description is rather detailed, but it seems necessary to explain the enormous pressure on Alwin Schockemöhle as he rode into the Bromont arena. One can only imagine what would have been the outcome if he had had the same bad luck as his brother Paul in the first round. Paul had been in brilliant form until he made a slight mistake and knocked down a pole. Then Talisman refused a jump and this led to a total of 24 faults against him. It's fairly safe to say that no one will ever again accuse Alwin Schockemöhle of having bad nerves!

About five years before his Olympic victory, the bay gelding, Warwick Rex had been for sale at a dealer's named Friedrich Ernst, in Verden on the river Aller. Hartwig Steenken bought him, but he didn't like him much and not long after he disposed of him to a Dutch rider, Melchior, who is certainly a great horselover and who has built himself an arena where he practises regularly. He has also entered for various major trials, but the fences seem to conspire against him, and you won't find his name in the tables of the more important winners.

Melchior passed the horse on to Hermann Schridde, who won the silver medal in the individual event at the 1964 Tokyo Olympics. Schridde has given up riding these days. His life is now flying and he specialises in taking up parachute jumpers. At some stage during the elimination trials he remarked: "At one time our aim was to enter for the major events and for this we prepared our horses very carefully. We didn't go chasing from one trial to another."

Perhaps if Hermann Schridde had been ten years younger and ten years more interested, he might have kept Warwick Rex for himself. After a while, he returned him to Melchior, who didn't care for him any more than he had done previously and sold him back to the original dealer in Verden. In 1974, Alwin Schockemöhle bought him and just over a year later, he won the European Championship with him. The year after that, they won the Olympic Gold Medal.

Alwin Schockemöhle says: "I wouldn't part with him for half a million marks!"

On the afternoon of July 27th 1976, which was late evening in Oldenburg, Germany, the church bells of Mühlen pealed out for Alwin Schockemöhle.

Appendix 1

SUMMARY OF A RIDER'S CAREER

Olympic Games

1960 Rome	Individual Event	26th with Ferdl
	Nations' Cup	Gold medal with Ferdl
1968 Mexico	Individual Event	7th with Donald Rex
	Nations' Cup	Bronze medal with Donald Rex
1976 Montreal	Individual Event	Gold medal with Warwick Rex
	Nations' Cup	Silver medal with Warwick Rex

World Championships

1970 La Baule	4th with Donald Rex
1974 Hickstead	Eliminated with Rex the Robber

European Championships

1961 Aachen	4th with Ferdl and Bacchus
1962 London	6th with Ferdl and Freiherr
1963 Rome	2nd with Ferdl and Freiherr
1965 Aachen	3rd with Exakt and Freiherr
1966 Lucerne	Eliminated with Exakt and Athlet
1967 Rotterdam	3rd with Donald Rex and Pesgö
1969 Hickstead	2nd with Donald Rex and Wimpel
1971 Aachen	Eliminated with Donald Rex and Wimpel
1973 Hickstead	2nd with Rex the Robber and Weiler
1975 Munich	European Champion with Warwick Rex

German Championships

1961 Berlin	German Champion with Freiherr
1963 Berlin	German Champion with Freiherr
1967 Berlin	German Champion with Donald Rex and Wimpel
1975 Berlin	German Champion with Warwick Rex and Rex the Robber

1.	1956	Stockholm	5th on Marsalla
2.	1957	Aachen	1st on Bacchus
3.	1959	Madrid	3rd on Partisan
4.		Geneva	3rd on Bacchus
5.	1960	Aachen	1st on Bacchus
6.		Rome (Olympic Games)	1st on Ferdl
7.	1961	Aachen	1st with Bacchus
8.		London	3rd with Freiherr
9.		Dublin	1st with Ferdl
10.		Rotterdam	2nd with Ferdl
11.		Geneva	1st with Ferdl
12.	1962	Lucerne	2nd with Ferdl
13.		Aachen	2nd with Ferdl
14.		London	1st with Ferdl
15.		Copenhagen	1st with Freiherr
16.		Rotterdam	1st with Ferdl
17.	1963	Rome	2nd with Ferdl
18.		Aachen	1st with Ferdl
19.		Dublin	2nd with Ferdl
20.		New York	3rd with Dämon
21.		Toronto	2nd with Dämon
22.	1964	Aachen	2nd with Freiherr
23.		Rotterdam	1st with Zukunft
24.	1965	Aachen	2nd with Exakt
25.		London	5th with Exakt
26.		Ostend	2nd with Zukunft
27.		Rotterdam	2nd with Exakt
28.		Geneva	3rd with Exakt
29.	1967	Aachen	5th with Donald Rex
30.		Rotterdam	2nd with Donald Rex
31.	1968	Aachen	3rd with Donald Rex
32.		Mexico (Olympic Games)	3rd with Donald Rex
33.	1969	Aachen	1st with Donald Rex
34.		London	1st with Donald Rex
35.		Dublin	1st with Donald Rex
36.		Geneva	1st with Donald Rex
37.	1970	Dublin	3rd with Donald Rex
38.	1971	Fontainebleau	1st with Donald Rex
39.	1972	Dublin	1st with Rex the Robber
40.		Rotterdam	1st with Rex the Robber
41.	1973	Aachen	1st with Rex the Robber
42.		London	1st with Rex the Robber
43.		Dublin	1st with Rex the Robber
44.		Rotterdam	1st with Rex the Robber
45.		Washington	3rd with Rex the Robber

46.		New York	2nd with Rex the Robber
47.		Toronto	2nd with Rex the Robber
48.	1974	La Baule	1st with Rex the Robber
49.		Dublin	2nd with Rex the Robber
50.		Rotterdam	3rd with Rex the Robber
51.		Aachen	1st with Rex the Robber
52		Lisbon	3rd with Warwick Rex
53	1975	Fontainebleau	4th with Rex the Robber
54		Aachen	1st with Warwick Rex
55.		Hickstead	2nd with Rex the Robber
56.		Rotterdam	1st with Warwick Rex
57.		Montreal (Olympic Games)	2nd with Warwick Rex

To which should be added 1st place in the Show Jumping Team at the 1975 Munich European Championship, riding Warwick Rex. Did not ride in the Nations' Cup events in 1958 or 1966.

Wins in important individual events (Grand Prix)

C.S.I.O. and C.S.I.

Aachen: Aachen Grand Prix
1962 with Freiherr
1968 with Donald Rex
1969 with Wimpel
Aachen: Europa Grand Prix
1960 with Bacchus
1973 with Rex the Robber
Aachen: International Jumping Championship of Germany
1969 with Donald Rex
1975 with Warwick Rex

Appendix 2

Aachen: Championship winner
1967 with Pesgö
1973 with Rex the Robber
Aachen: N.R.W. Prize
1957 with Marsalla
1961 with Ferdl
Amsterdam: Amsterdam Grand Prix
1965 with Exakt
1966 with Athlet
1971 with Rex the Robber
1972 with Rex the Robber
Amsterdam: Netherlands' Grand Prix
1972 with Weiler
Berlin: German Grand Prix
1963 with Freiherr
1969 with Donald Rex
Berlin: Berlin Bear
1968 with Wimpel
1970 with Wimpel
Berlin: Winners' Prize
1968 with Donald Rex
Brussels: Brussels Grand Prix
1967 with Wimpel
1968 with Donald Rex
Cardiff: Amateur Championship
1974 (No horse mentioned)
Dortmund: German Federal Republic Grand Prix
1968 with Donald Rex
1973 with Rex the Robber
Dortmund: Dortmund Championship
1962 with Freiherr
1967 with Athlet
1968 with Donald Rex
1973 with Rex the Robber
Dinard: Dinard Grand Prix

1970 with Donald Rex
Donaueschingen: Prinz Kari Prize
1975 with Warwick Rex
Dublin: Puissance
1963 with Ferdl
1970 with Wimpel
Dublin: Irish Trophy (Grand Prix)
1972 with Rex the Robber
Fontainebleau: Fontainebleau Grand Prix
1969 with Donald Rex
1971 with Donald Rex
Frankfurt: Frankfurt Grand Prix
1963 with Freiherr
1964 with Freiherr
1967 with Pesgö
1970 with Donald Rex
Hanover: Hanover Grand Prix
1963 with Freiherr
1964 with Freiherr
Hickstead: Embassy Masters
1975 with Warwick Rex and Rex the Robber
Hertogenbosch: Hertogenbosch Grand Prix
1970 with Donald Rex
Hamburg: German Jumping Derby
1957 with Bacchus
1969 with Wimpel
1971 with Wimpel
The Hague: Hague Grand Prix
1972 with Rex the Robber
Cologne: Cologne Grand Prix
1965 with Freiherr
Lisbon: Lisbon Grand Prix
1974 with Warwick Rex
Lisbon: Victor Ludorum
1974 with Warwick Rex
London: King George V Gold Cup
1975 with Rex the Robber
London: John Player Trophy (Grand Prix)
1969 with Donald Rex
1975 with Rex the Robber
Ludwigsburg: Ludwigsburg Grand Prix
1964 with Freiherr
1969 with Wimpel
1970 with Donald Rex
Rome: Bettoni Prize (Puissance)
1963 with Ferdl

Rotterdam: Rotterdam Grand Prix
1973 with Rex the Robber
St Gallen: Dunhill Trophy
1975 with Rex the Robber
Washington: The President of the U.S. Trophy
1973 with Rex the Robber
Wolfsburg: Golden Beetle (Grand Prix)
1968 with Wimpel
Wiesbaden: Wiesbaden Casino Grand Prix
1969 with Donald Rex
1970 with Donald Rex